The material in this book does not consitute medical advice. It is intended for informational purposes only. The authors take no responsibility for the reader following the information in this book. Please consult your doctor for specific recommendations regarding your specific renal diet.

Before taking any course of treatment, please seek the advice of a physician or healthcare provider. The following recipes are specific for Chronic Kidney Disease (CKD). Due to variations in ingredients, the nutritional analysis should be used as guidelines, and we cannot guarantee the accuracy of all values.

Introduction

This extraordinary cookbook contains recipes from around the world. After three Mama Lolo's Cookbooks, authors Pauline and Lolo have grown in perfecting the ULTIMATE cookbook for families striving for better ways to eat living on a restricted diet. It is important to note that many of these traditional dishes are adapted to be kidney-friendly.

Easy-to-make recipes with full color, taste-tempting pictures are even more fun to read with the corresponding flag of the country on each page.

Travel with us through the world on a culinary journey to delight your senses and provide a unique gustatory experience.

Watch for more of your favorite countries in our next edition of the International Kidney Disease Cookbook!

More from Mama Lolo's Cookbooks...
Avalable on Amazon.com & Barnesandnoble.com

  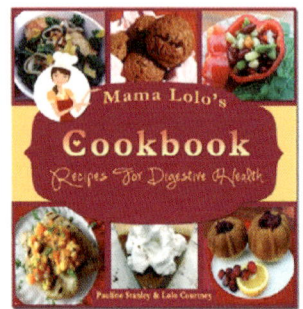

About The Authors...

Throughout our lives we have periods where we are close to our families, especially in times of need. All families go through their ups and downs. Often times illnesses bring families together as was the case in our family. This was the inspiration needed to write this book when our family member was diagnosed with End Stage Renal Disease (ESRD).

Lolo, being a nurse of 30+ years and Pauline, being a fabulous homecook along with the added benefit of having a graphic design background, decided to collaborate in this venture. Thus was born Mama Lolo's Cookbooks and our latest book ... The International Kidney Disease Cookbook.

Anyone living on a restricted diet knows how difficult it is to travel. If you are living on dialysis, having to work with this can be a daunting task. Finding foods that you are able to eat while traveling can really be troublesome. This cookbook will help in this endeavor in learning about the kidney-friendly foods of different countries.

We hope these recipes will take you on a journey that will delight your tastebuds making each meal a trip that you will never forget.

Leaching or Dialysing Vegetables

Potatoes, carrots, sweet potatoes and beets are a staple in so many diets around the world. It is hard enough to eat a renal diet, let alone having to eliminate such hearty vegetables as these. Leaching the veggies can pull some of the potassium out of them, but be careful and check with your dietician as to how much is OK on your diet.

Directions:

1. Peel and slice the vegetables into small pieces.
2. Using 10x the amount of water per amount of veggie, soak the vegetables for two hours.
3. Drain and repeat the process of soaking.
4. Cook with 5x the amount of water to the amount of vegetables.

Table Of Contents

7 | Mexico

29 | USA

59 | Italy

75 | Spain

93 | Greece

103 | Lebanon

113 | England

125 | India

135 | China

149 | Vietnam

161 | Thailand

Mexico

Food in Mexico, along with the people, have a long rich history. Some believe that it's authentic foods may have come from the Mayan Indians, followed by the influences of the Aztec Empire in the mid 1300's. Corn tortillas, chili peppers and many different herbs and spices are commonly found in this cultures culinary traditions.

9 | Esparragos con Salsa

11 | Ensalada de Pollo

13 | Jicama Chips

15 | Savory Cilantro Arroz

17 | Salsa 3 Ways - Chili Pablano

18 | Salsa 3 Ways - Grilled Corn Salsa

19 | Salsa 3 Ways - Jicama Salsa

21 | Tostada Grande

23 | Jicama Slaw

25 | Camarones con Salsa Roja

27 | Mexicana Tacos de Pescado

Esparragos con Salsa

Serves: 4
Prep Time: 5 min.
Cooking Time: 10 min.

1. In a bowl, mix the mustard, honey mayonnaise and mustard seed.
2. Season the mixture abundantly with black pepper and set aside.
3. Cut off and discard the hard stems from the asparagus spears.
4. In boiling water, cook the asparagus for 9 minutes and drain.
5. Place spears in serving bowl and cover with the mustard sauce.
6. Serve immediately.

2 bunches green asparagus

4 tbsp. mustard

2 tbsp. honey

2 tbsp. light mayonnaise

1 tbsp. mustard seeds

ground black pepper

Super Saludable!

Percent Daily Values (DV) are based on a 2000 calorie diet.

Calories	66.1	Protein	2.9g
Total Fats	2.2g	Potassium	95.9mg
Sodium	231.7mg	Phosphorus	1.2%

9 | MEXICO

Ensalada de Pollo

Serves: 6
Prep Time: 15 min.
Cooking Time: -

1. On a large serving platter or individual plate, layer all the ingredients.
2. Top with the cotija cheese and white corn tortilla stips.
4. For an added bonus, top with one of our salsas (pg. 17, 18, 19) for a great dressing!

Hope you enjoy!

4 c. shredded lettuce

1 1/2 c. cubed deli rotisserie chicken (without skin)

1/4 c. shredded red cabbage

1/2 c. diced red pepper

1/4 c. chopped cilantro

4 oz. cotija cheese

1/2 c. white corn tortilla strips, unsalted

Percent Daily Values (DV) are based on a 2000 calorie diet.

Calories	146.8	Protein	10.3g
Total Fats	7.2g	Potassium	132.4mg
Sodium	311.2mg	Phosphorus	8.2%

11 | MEXICO

Jicama Chips

Serves: 12
Prep Time: 15 min.
Cooking Time: 30 min.

1. Preheat oven to 400 F.
2. Peel and slice the jicama into thin slices (mandolin works great).
3. Mix all the powdered spices in a small bowl.
4. In large bowl, combine jicama slices and spice mixture. Toss to coat.
5. On a lined cookie sheet, spread out slices evenly.
6. Coat with cooking spray.
7. Place in oven for 25-30 minutes, or until crisp.
8. Remove from oven and enjoy!

> I could eat these everyday!

3 whole fresh jicamas
1 tbsp. chili powder
1 tbsp. garlic powder
1 tbsp. onion powder
cooking spray

Percent Daily Values (DV) are based on a 2000 calorie diet.

Calories	68.8	Protein	1.4g
Total Fats	0.3g	Potassium	271.9mg
Sodium	13.4mg	Phosphorus	3.6%

13 | MEXICO

Savory Cilantro Arroz

Serves: 4
Prep Time: 10 min.
Cooking Time: 45 min.

1. Heat the oil in a pan over medium heat.
2. Add the leeks and sauté until tender, about 10 minutes.
3. Add the garlic and sauté for 1 minute.
4. Add the rice and toast for 3 minutes.
5. Add the water, bring to a boil, reduce heat to simmer, cover and cook for 18-20 minutes.
6. Remove from heat, fluff with a fork and mix in cilantro, lime juice, and zest.

1 tbsp. canola oil
1/2 c. chopped leeks
1 garlic clove, chopped
1 c. long grain white rice
2 c. water
1 handful cilantro, chopped
1 lime (juice & zest)

Olé!!!!

Percent Daily Values (DV) are based on a 2000 calorie diet

Calories	92.5	Protein	1.3g
Total Fats	3.6g	Potassium	50.4mg
Sodium	3.0mg	Phosphorus	2.3%

Salsa 3 Ways - Chili Poblano

Serves: 10
Prep Time: 15 min.
Cooking Time: -

1. Using a blender or a food processor, blend the green peppers with the cilantro and poblanos until smooth.
2. Add the cream cheese and blend until smooth.
3. Blend in chicken broth and oil while blender is still running.
4. Add the lime juice, garlic powder, and pepper. Blend until smooth.
5. Refrigerate until ready to use.

Espeso y cremoso!

1 green pepper, seeded, quartered
1 handful cilantro
3 poblano chilies, roasted, peeled, seeded
3 oz. light cream cheese
2 tbsp. low-sodium chicken broth
2 tbsp. canola oil
1 tbsp. fresh lime juice
1/2 tsp. garlic powder
pepper to taste

Percent Daily Values (DV) are based on a 2000 calorie diet

Calories	49.5	Protein	1.0g
Total Fats	3.3g	Potassium	10.3mg
Sodium	31.4mg	Phosphorus	0%

Salsa 3 Ways - Grilled Corn Salsa

Serves: 6
Prep Time: 15 min.
Cooking Time: 10 min.

1. Preheat your grill to the highest setting.
2. Generously coat the corn with oil and sprinkle lightly with chili powder and pepper.
3. Grill the corn on all sides 4-5 minutes.
4. With a sharp knife, cut corn kernels from the cob and set aside.
5. In a skillet, sauté the onion in oil over medium heat for 2 minutes (do not brown).
6. Remove onion from heat and place in medium-sized serving bowl.
7. Add corn, bell pepper, and serrano chilies. Season with lime juice and pepper. Mix well.
8. Refrigerate until ready to use.

Deliciosamente colorido!

4 ears fresh corn on the cob
1 tsp. chili powder
1 c. diced onion
2 tsp. canola oil
1 red bell pepper, seeded, diced
2 serrano chilies, seeded, diced
fresh lime juice
pepper to taste

Percent Daily Values (DV) are based on a 2000 calorie diet

Calories	81.4	Protein	2.3g
Total Fats	2.2g	Potassium	202.7mg
Sodium	10.0mg	Phosphorus	5.4%

Salsa 3 Ways - Jicama Salsa

Serves: 8
Prep Time: 15 min.
Cooking Time: -

1. Thinly slice jicama and then cut into 1/4" dice.
2. Core and seed pepper and cut into 1/4" dice.
3. Combine the rest of ingredients in a large bowl, add jicama and pepper, toss well.
4. Refrigerate 1 hour and serve.

3 medium jicama, peeled
1 red bell pepper
juice from 1 lemon
1/4 c. rice wine vinegar
pepper to taste
minced fresh cilantro

Super simple and tasty!

Percent Daily Values (DV) are based on a 2000 calorie diet

Calories	73.9	Protein	1.3g
Total Fats	0.1g	Potassium	247.1mg
Sodium	96.6mg	Phosphorus	3.0%

19 | MEXICO

Tostada Grande

Serves: 16
Prep Time: 10 min.
Cooking Time: 9 min.

1. Preheat oven to 350°F.
2. Place the flour tortillas directly on the rack in oven and bake for 4 minutes to toast (tortillas will not be crisp).
3. Combine onion, chicken, chilies, and butter in a medium bowl. Mix well.
4. Coat a pizza pan or stone with cooking spray.
5. Put one tortilla on the pan, and top with the chicken mixture. Sprinkle with pepper and chili powder.
6. Top with the second tortilla.
7. Repeat process with remaining tortillas.
8. Bake for 5 minutes.
9. Meanwhile, combine cheeses in a small bowl.
10. Remove the tortillas from the oven and top with cheese mixture.
11. Garnish with chopped lettuce, cojita, and mozzarella.

Caliente! Hot and creamy!

4 burrito-sized flour tortillas

1 1/2 c. cooked, shredded chicken

1/4 tsp. chili powder

2 oz. fat-free cream cheese

1/2 c. low-fat ricotta cheese

pepper

2 tbsp. romano cheese

1 c. onion, diced

1 4 1/2 oz. can diced green chilies

1 tbsp. unsalted butter

2 oz. crumbled cotija cheese

1 c. romaine lettuce, chopped

3 oz. low fat mozzarella cheese, shredded

Percent Daily Values (DV) are based on a 2000 calorie diet

Calories	160.9	Protein	9.5g
Total Fats	2.7g	Potassium	90.1mg
Sodium	139.1mg	Phosphorus	7.6%

21 | MEXICO

Jicama Slaw

Serves: 8
Prep Time: 20 min.
Cooking Time: -

1. Place jicama, celery, peppers and cucumber in a large bowl.
2. In a small bowl, whisk together the lime juice, vinegar, ancho powder, honey and oil.
3. Season with pepper to taste.
4. Pour the dressing over the jicama mixture and toss to coat well.
5. Fold in the cilantro, let stand at room temperature for 20 minutes before serving.

Crujiente y tan delicioso!

1 large jicama, peeled and shredded
1 cucumber, deseeded, partially peeled, cubed
1 c. celery, diced
1 red pepper, deseeded, diced
1/2 c. fresh lime juice
2 tbsp. rice vinegar
2 tbsp. ancho chili powder
2 tbsp. honey
1/2 c. canola oil
pepper to taste
1/4 c. cilantro leaves, diced

Percent Daily Values (DV) are based on a 2000 calorie diet

Calories	207.5	Protein	1.4g
Total Fats	13.8g	Potassium	296.6mg
Sodium	79.6mg	Phosphorus	3.2%

Camarones con Salsa Roja

Serves: 6
Prep Time: 10 min.
Cooking Time: 5 min.

1. In a large sauté pan, heat the olive oil over medium heat.
2. Lower the heat and add the garlic and red pepper flakes. Sauté for 1 minute.
3. Add all of the ingredients but the parsley, and cook for 3 minutes or until shrimp are pink.
4. Transfer to serving plate and top with parsley.
5. Serve with white rice if desired.

Mariscos deleite!

10 oz. large shrimp, peeled, deveined

1 roasted red pepper, pureed

3 cloves garlic, minced

1 tsp. paprika

1 tsp. red pepper flakes

4 oz. white wine

2 tbsp. extra virgin olive oil

juice of 2 lemons

3 tbsp. fresh parsley, chopped

1/2 c. sliced jalapenos

Percent Daily Values (DV) are based on a 2000 calorie diet

Calories	68.5	Protein	10.2g
Total Fats	0.5g	Potassium	117.4mg
Sodium	148.7mg	Phosphorus	7.0%

25 | MEXICO

Mexicana Tacos de Pescado

Serves: 4
Prep Time: 15 min.
Cooking Time: 15 min.

1. Thaw fish if frozen, pat dry.
2. In a bowl combine oregano, flour, cumin, and cayenne.
3. Add the fish and toss gently to coat.
4. Spray a skillet with cooking spray and heat over medium heat.
5. Add fish in an even layer and cook on each side, 3-5 minutes or until fish flakes easily with a fork.
6. In a small bowl combine sour cream and lime zest.
7. In another bowl combine cabbage, onions, cilantro and peppers.
8. To assemble, place fish on each corn tortilla and top with sour cream mixture and cabbage mixture.

Voy a tomar dos!

8 oz. fresh or frozen skinless red snapper filets
1/2 tsp. oregano
1/2 tsp. cumin
1/4 c. white flour
1/8 tsp. cayenne pepper
3 cloves garlic, minced
1/3 c. light sour cream
1 tsp. lime zest
1 1/2 c. napa cabbage, finely shredded
6 tbsp. onion, chopped
3 tbsp. cilantro, chopped
1/2 c. red pepper, diced
8 - 6" corn tortillas, warmed

Percent Daily Values (DV) are based on a 2000 calorie diet

Calories	123.1	Protein	15.6g
Total Fats	2.1g	Potassium	81.1mg
Sodium	41.7mg	Phosphorus	2.0%

27 | MEXICO

USA

Early American cuisine was heavily influenced by the European colonization of the Americas as well as the traditional foods of the American Indians. These days, food from the US has truely become a fusion of tastes from around the world.

31 | Baked Fish and Asparagus

33 | Spicy Grilled Watermelon

35 | Creamy Shrimp and Cucumbers

37 | Pork Chops and Roasted Apples

39 | Fancy Crab Cakes

41 | New England Fish Cakes

43 | Hawaiian Shoyu Chicken

45 | Skinny Cajun Chicken Linguine

47 | Vermont Oatmeal Cookies

49 | Blueberry Zucchini Coffeecake

51 | Cowboy Cookies

53 | California Chai Cupcakes

55 | Red, White & Blue Parfait

57 | All-American Blueberry Pie

Baked Fish and Asparagus

Serves: 4
Prep Time: 10 min.
Cooking Time: 20 min.

1. Preheat the oven to 350°F.
2. Take the juice from 1 lemon and pour over the fish in a shallow dish.
3. Refrigerate for 15 minutes to marinate.
4. In two separate bowls, place the beaten egg in one, and the breadcrumbs in the other.
5. Take the marinated fish filets and dip first in the egg, followed by the breadcrumb mixture until well coated.
6. Place the fish filets on a lined baking sheet.
7. In a large bowl coat the asparagus in canola oil and place on the baking sheet with the fish.
9. Place in the oven for 12-15 minutes, or until fish flakes easily with a fork and is nicely browned.
10. Serve the remaining lemon juice with the fish and asparagus.

4 tilapia filets
1 c. Italian breadcrumbs
1/2 c. panko breadcrumbs
1 egg
2 tbsp. canola oil
juice from 2 lemons
1 lb. fresh asparagus spears, trimmed

Percent Daily Values (DV) are based on a 2000 calorie diet

Calories	203	Protein	14.3g
Total Fats	7.9g	Potassium	234.3mg
Sodium	359.4mg	Phosphorus	1.6%

31 | USA

Spicy Grilled Watermelon

Serves: 24
Prep Time: 10 min.
Cooking Time: 4 min.

1. Slice the watermelon into 1" thick wedges.
2. In a small bowl combine lime zest, lime juice, half of the honey and chili-garlic sauce. Mix well and set aside.
3. With a paper towel, pat dry the watermelon pieces to soak up any excess water.
4. Drizzle the remaining honey onto the watermelon slices.
5. Heat a grill pan over high heat, and grill the watermelon on each side for 1-2 minutes or until nice grill marks are formed.
6. Remove watermelon from grill and place in a large serving bowl.
7. Pour the lime mixture over the watermelon, and top with the chopped cilantro.

A family favorite!

zest of 1 small lime
juice of 2 limes
1/4 c. honey
2 tbsp. chili-garlic sauce
1 medium watermelon, seedless
2 tbsp. fresh cilantro

Percent Daily Values (DV) are based on a 2000 calorie diet

Calories	71.4	Protein	1.3g
Total Fats	0.9g	Potassium	222.2mg
Sodium	7.3mg	Phosphorus	1.8%

33 | USA

Creamy Shrimp and Cucumbers

Serves: 6
Prep Time: 15 min.
Cooking Time: -

1. In a large bowl, combine sour cream, mayonnaise, lime juice and Old Bay.
2. Add shrimp, celery, cucumbers and mix.
3. Refrigerate.
4. Meanwhile, scoop sliced cucumber centers out with a melon baller or spoon.
5. When ready to serve, remove shrimp mixture from refrigerator and fill cucumbers.
6. Serve and enjoy!

Delightful appetizer!

10 oz. medium cooked shrimp, peeled, deveined
2 medium cucumbers, peeled, sliced 1"
1 large celery stalk, sliced thin
1/4 c. low-fat sour cream
2 tbsp. light mayonnaise
2 tbsp. lime juice
1 tsp. Old Bay seasoning

Percent Daily Values (DV) are based on a 2000 calorie diet

Calories	78.0	Protein	10.3g
Total Fats	2.9g	Potassium	137.0mg
Sodium	162.7mg	Phosphorus	7.8%

Pork Chops and Roasted Apples

Serves: 4
Prep Time: 10 min.
Cooking Time: 45 min.

1. Preheat oven to 350°F.
1. On a large, lined baking sheet, place the pork chops down and season both sides with the thyme, pepper, garlic powder, and onion powder.
2. Take the sliced apples and spread out evenly on top of the pork chops.
3. Place in the oven and bake for 45 minutes or until the pork is cooked (160 F).
4. Remove from oven, cover pork and set aside.
5. Take the roasted apples and place them in a small saucepan.
6. Add the butter, brown sugar and cinnamon.
7. Cover and let simmer over medium-low heat, stirring occasionally for 5-7 minutes or until apples are soft.
8. Serve alongside or on top of your pork chops.

A classic American dish!

2 large pork chops, fat removed
1 tsp. thyme
1 tsp. black pepper
1 tbsp. garlic powder
1 tsp. onion powder
2 tbsp. unsalted butter
2 apples, sliced
1 tsp. brown sugar, packed
1 tsp. cinnamon

Percent Daily Values (DV) are based on a 2000 calorie diet

Calories	118.8	Protein	11.4g
Total Fats	4.5g	Potassium	222.4mg
Sodium	25.5mg	Phosphorus	11.7%

37 | USA

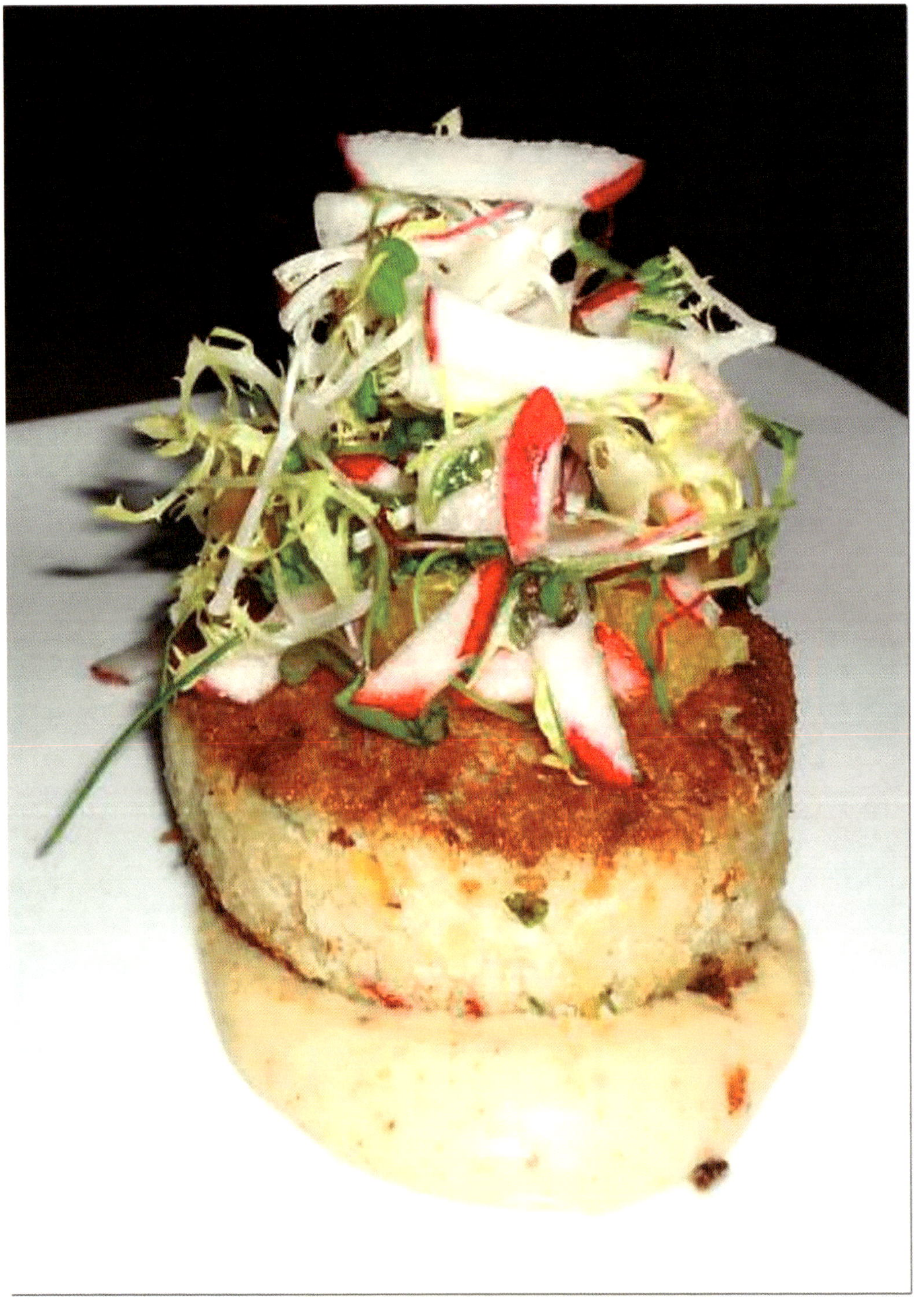

Fancy Crab Cakes

Serves: 4
Prep Time: 20 min.
Cooking Time: 20 min.

1. Preheat oven to 400°F.
2. Coat a baking sheet with nonstick cooking spray.
3. In a large bowl, mix together the egg, mustard, Worcestershire sauce, lemon juice, Old Bay, and hot sauce!
4. Stir in the bell pepper and scallion.
5. Gently fold in the crab, 1/4 cup of bread crumbs and pepper to taste.
6. Put the remaining breadcrumbs in a shallow dish.
7. Divide the crab mixture into 8 mounds.
8. Shape the mounds into rounds and coat in breadcrumbs.
9. Transfer to prepared baking sheet and flatten the patties so they are about 1" high.
10. Bake until golden on bottom, about 10 minutes.
11. Flip the crab cakes and continue to bake for 10 minutes.
12. For tartar sauce, combine all ingredients and spoon on plate and top with crab cakes.

1 egg lightly beaten
2 tsp. Dijon mustard
1 tsp. Worcestershire sauce
1 tbsp. fresh lemon juice
1 tsp. lemon zest
dash of hot sauce
1/2 tsp. Old Bay
1/2 cup red bell pepper, chopped
1 scallion, chopped
1 lb. lump crab, picked over for shells
3/4 cup bread crumbs
black pepper

Tartar Sauce:
6 tbsp. nonfat plain greek yogurt
2 tbsp. light mayonnaise
1 scallion, finely chopped
1/2 tsp. chopped capers

••• Garnish with frisée, radishes, and lemon wedges

Percent Daily Values (DV) are based on a 2000 calorie diet

Calories	76.1	Protein	14.1g
Total Fats	1.7g	Potassium	254.7mg
Sodium	301.6mg	Phosphorus	10.2%

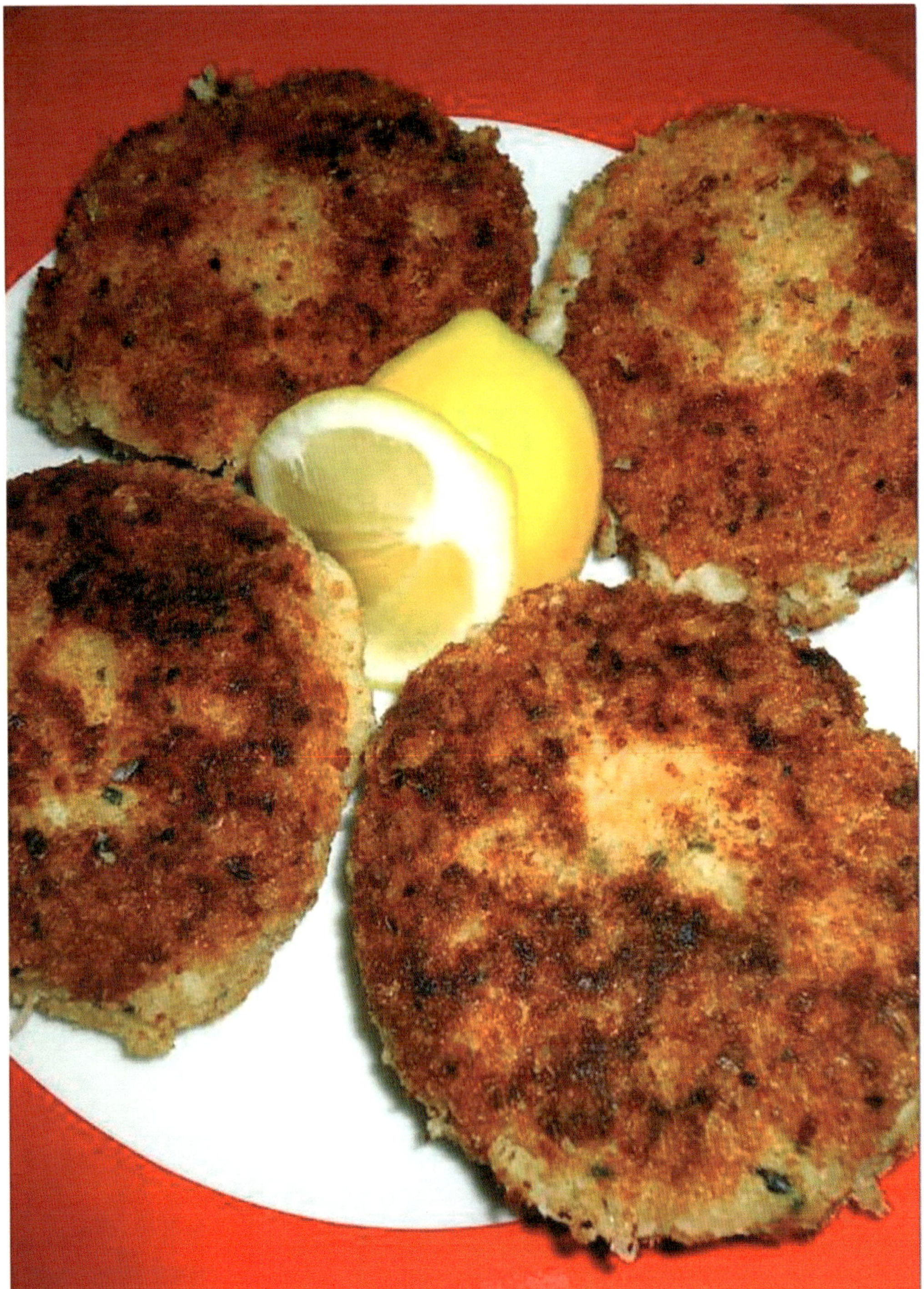

New England Fish Cakes

Serves: 6
Prep Time: 15 min.
Cooking Time: 15 min.

1. Preheat oven to 425°F.
2. Place fish in a sauté pan with 1/2 cup of water.
3. Cover and cook on medium heat for 5-6 minutes or until fish flakes easily.
4. Drain the water, remove fish, and use fork to break into small pieces.
5. In a large bowl, add the onion, egg whites, parsley, panko, mustard and fish.
6. Mix well.
7. Form into patties and place on a lined baking sheet.
8. Bake for 10 minutes or until each side is lightly browned.

Bring the coast to your dinner table!

- 3 cod filets
- 1/2 medium onion, chopped
- 2 egg whites
- 3/4 c. panko breadcrumbs
- 1 tbsp. parsley, chopped
- 1 tbsp. Dijon mustard

Percent Daily Values (DV) are based on a 2000 calorie diet

Calories	94.2	Protein	12.3g
Total Fats	1.2g	Potassium	261.6mg
Sodium	134.8mg	Phosphorus	10.3%

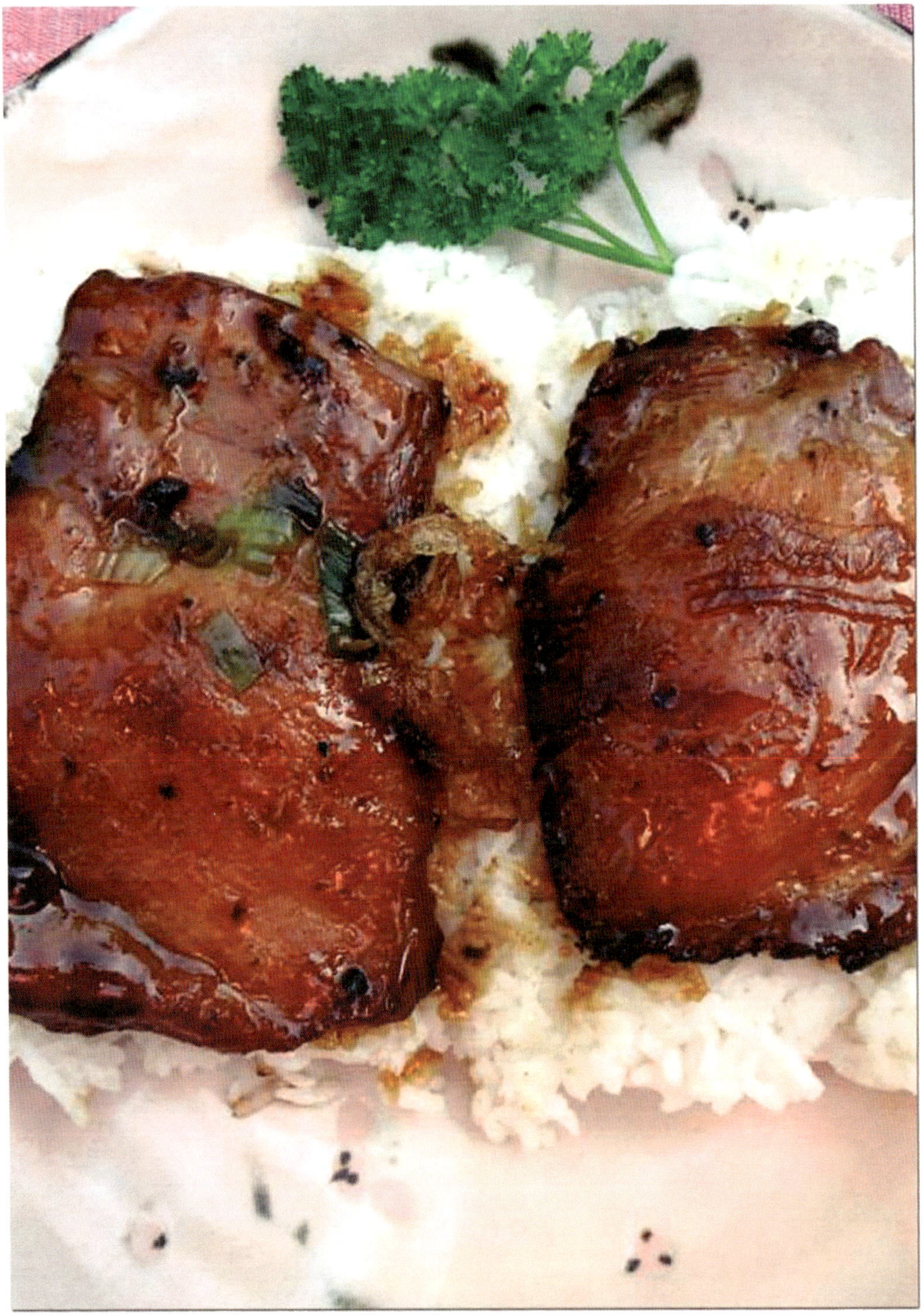

Hawaiian Shoyu Chicken

Serves: 10
Prep Time: 10 min.
Cooking Time: 45 min.

1. Combine all ingredients except for the cornstarch and scallions in a large stock pot.
2. Bring to a boil over high heat.
3. Reduce to low and simmer, stirring occasionally, until chicken is tender, about 45 minutes.
4. Remove chicken to a serving platter.
5. Bring remaining stock to a boil, skim off excess fat, and cook until reduced, about 20 minutes.
6. Whisk in cornstarch mixture.
7. Add the chicken back to the pot and stir to coat.
8. Serve chicken over the white rice and garnish with sliced scallions.

A tropical treat!

- 10 chicken thighs
- 4 c. low-sodium fat-free chicken broth
- 2 tbsp. low-sodium soy sauce
- 1/4 c. light brown sugar, packed
- 1 oz. mirin
- 2 garlic cloves, peeled, smashed
- 4" piece of ginger, sliced 1/2" thick, smashed
- 1 tsp. black pepper
- 3 tbsp. cornstarch, dissolved in 5 tbsp. water
- 10 c. long grain white rice, cooked
- sliced scallions for garnish

Percent Daily Values (DV) are based on a 2000 calorie diet

Calories	243.7	Protein	4.9g
Total Fats	0.4g	Potassium	76.5mg
Sodium	320.7mg	Phosphorus	7.1%

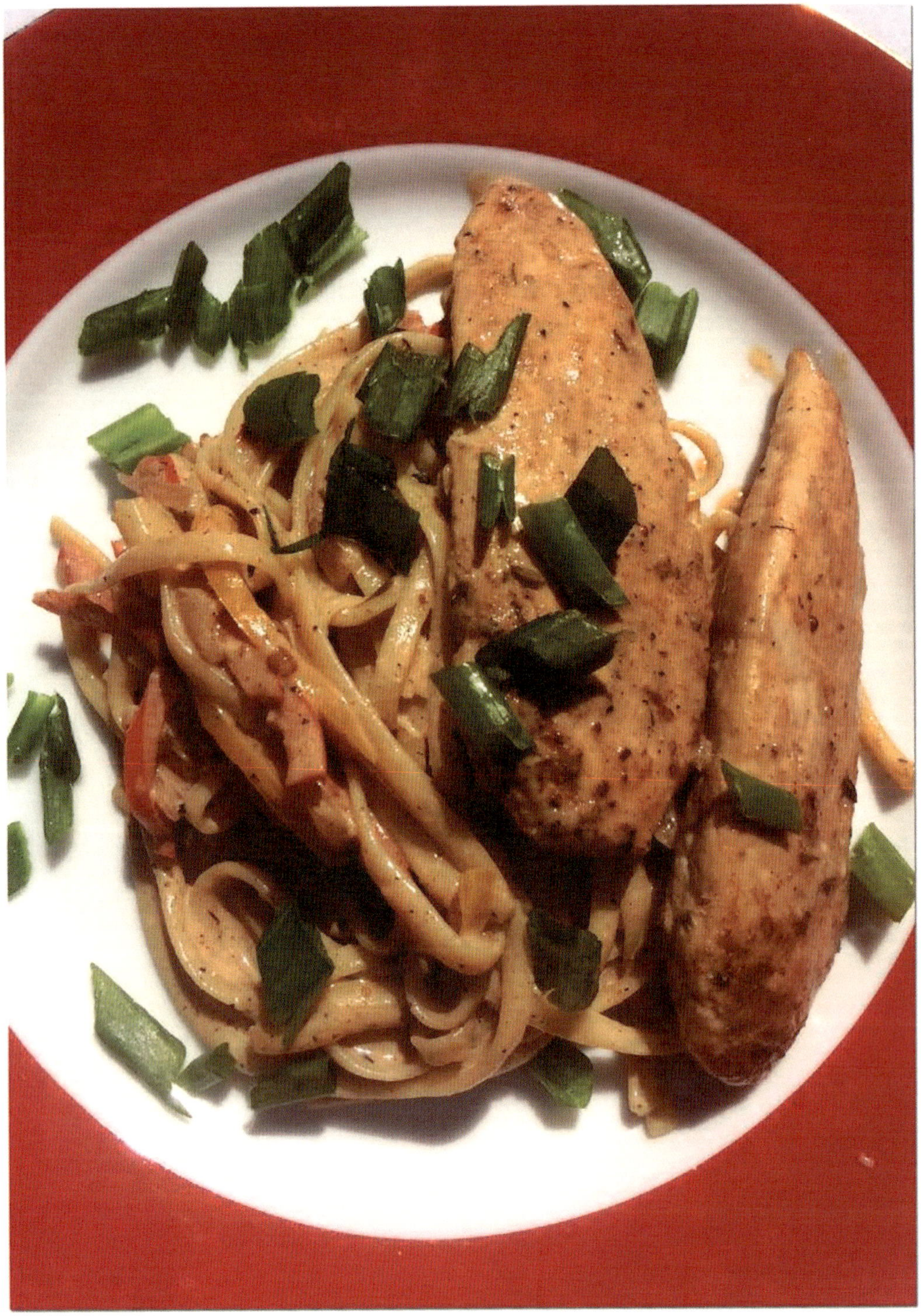

Skinny Cajun Chicken Linguine

Serves: 5
Prep Time: 20 min.
Cooking Time: 30 min.

1. In a small blender, combine almond milk, flour and cream cheese until smooth, set aside.
2. Season the chicken on both sides with Cajun seasoning and garlic powder.
3. Prepare the pasta in non-salted water according to package directions.
4. Heat a large skillet over medium-high heat.
5. Spray the pan with cooking spray and sauté the chicken for 5-6 minutes or until no longer pink.
6. Remove from pan and set aside.
7. Reduce the heat to medium and add the olive oil to the skillet.
8. Add the peppers, onions, garlic and sauté for 8 minutes.
9. Season with garlic powder and black pepper to taste.
10. Reduce the heat to medium low, add the chicken broth, then pour in the milk mixture and continue stirring for two minutes.
11. Add the chicken and linguine to the pan and toss to coat.
12. Top with chopped scallions.

8 oz. uncooked linguine

1 lb. chicken breast strips

2 tsp. Cajun seasoning

1 tbsp. garlic powder

1 tbsp. olive oil

1 medium red bell pepper, sliced thin

1 medium yellow bell pepper, sliced thin

1/2 red onion, chopped

3 cloves garlic, minced

1 c. fat-free low-sodium chicken broth

1/3 c. almond milk

1 tbsp. flour

3 tbsp. non-dairy light cream cheese

black pepper

2 scallions, chopped

Percent Daily Values (DV) are based on a 2000 calorie diet

Calories	236.4	Protein	10.9g
Total Fats	5.2g	Potassium	115.6mg
Sodium	288.2mg	Phosphorus	3.7%

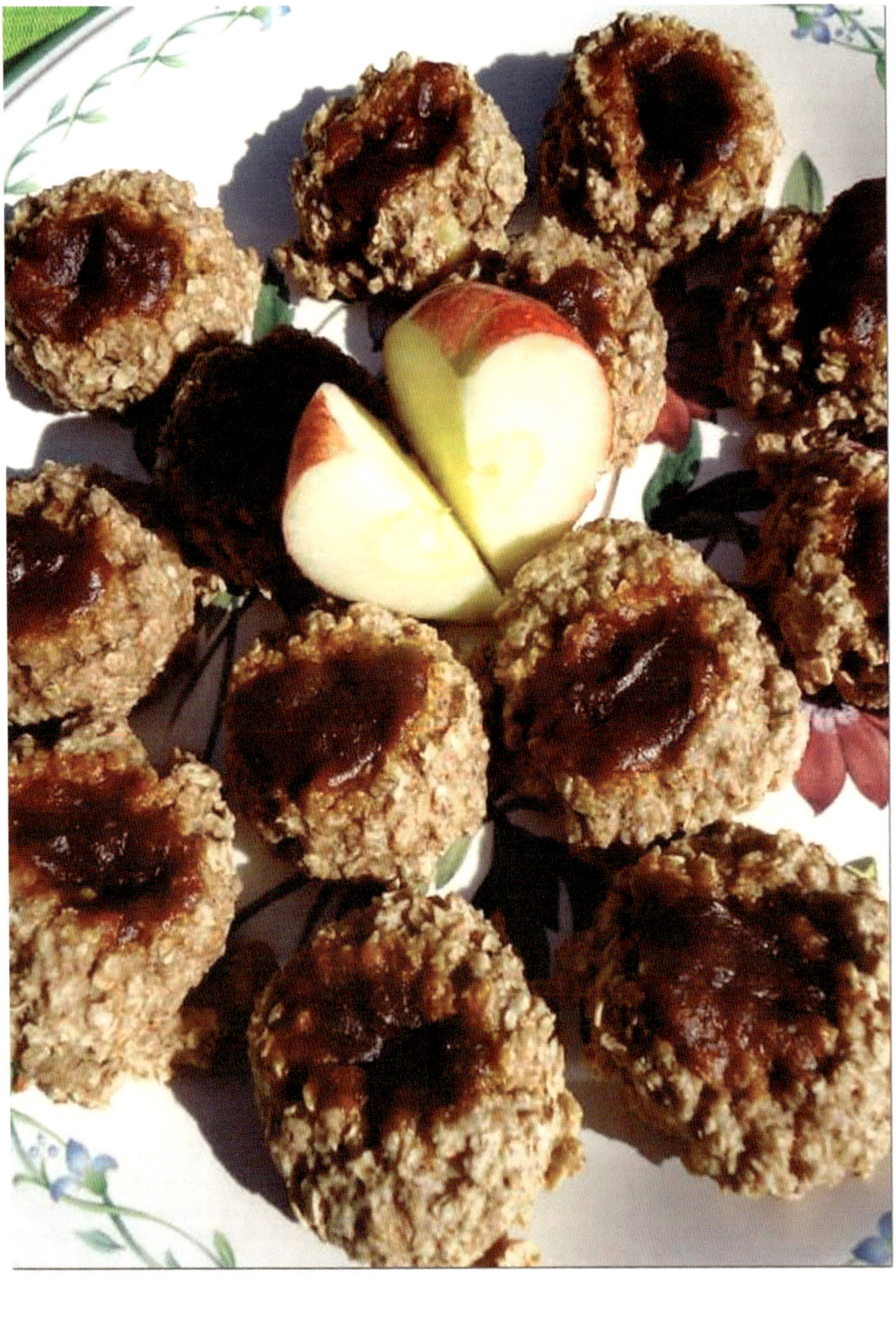

Vermont Oatmeal Cookies

Serves: 12
Prep Time: 20 min.
Cooking Time: 8-10 min.

1. Preheat oven to 350°F.
2. Line one baking sheet with parchment paper.
3. In medium bowl, combine flour, oats, baking soda and cream of tartar, stirring with a whisk.
4. In a large bowl, combine sugar and butter with a hand mixer until creamy and smooth.
5. Add the honey, vanilla and egg. Blend well.
6. Gradually add the flour mixture to the sugar mixture blending just until combined.
7. Cover and chill for 10 minutes.
8. Remove dough from the refrigerator, and with moist hands, shape into 12 balls.
9. Place balls 2" apart on baking sheet and slightly flatten with a fork.
10. Place a dollop of applesauce in the center of each ball.
11. Bake for 8-10 minutes (cookies will be slightly soft).
12. Let cool and serve!

- 1 c. white flour
- 1/2 c. rolled oats
- 1/2 tsp. baking soda
- 1/2 tsp. cream of tartar
- 1 c. sugar
- 1/4 c. unsalted butter, softened
- 1 tbsp. honey
- 1 tsp. vanilla
- 1 large egg
- 4 oz. cinnamon applesauce

Percent Daily Values (DV) are based on a 2000 calorie diet

Calories	170.3	Protein	2.2g
Total Fats	4.7g	Potassium	47.3mg
Sodium	60.0mg	Phosphorus	2.2%

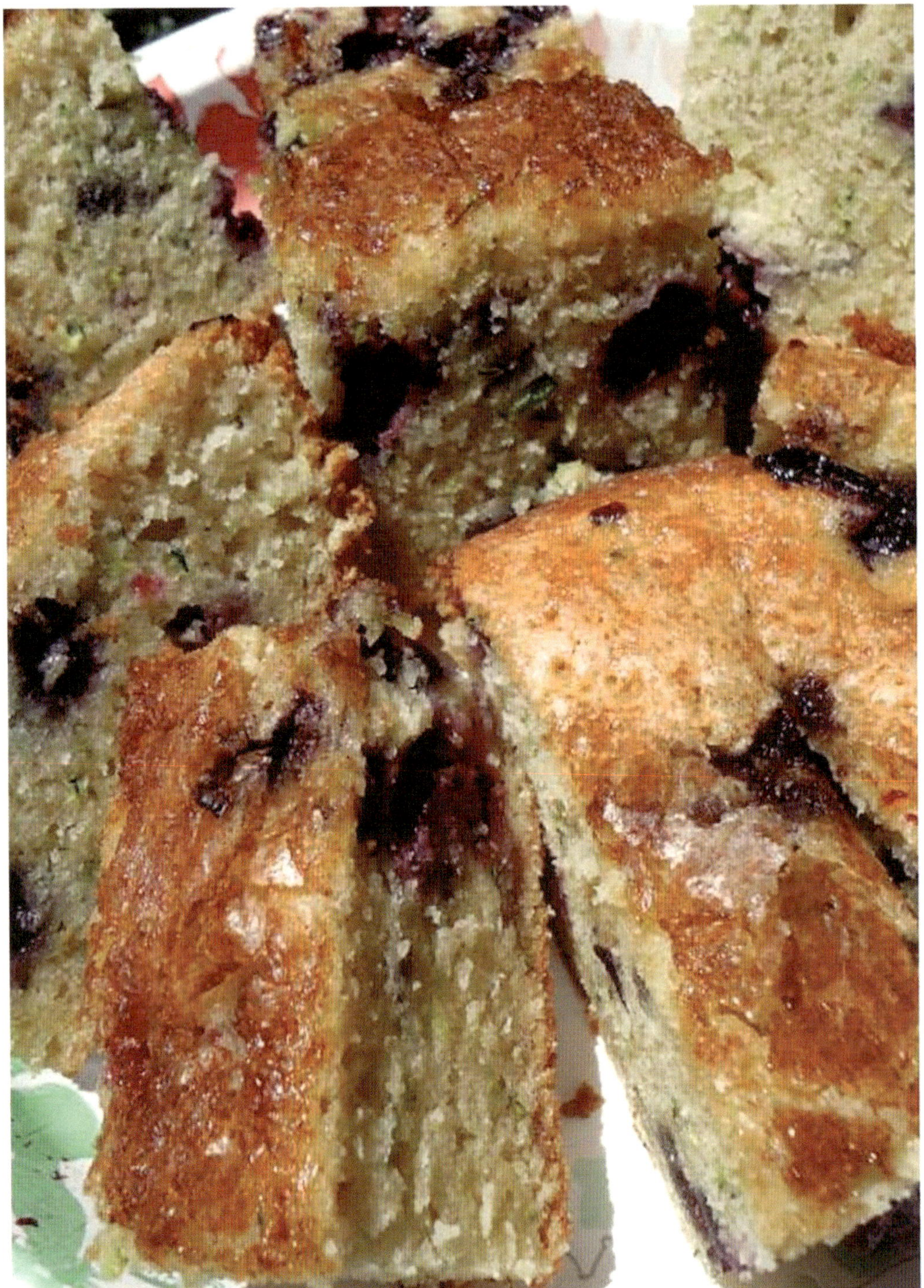

Blueberry Zucchini Coffeecake

Serves: 12
Prep Time: 15 min.
Cooking Time: 20 min.

1. Preheat oven to 350°F.
2. Combine flour, sugar, baking powder, cinnamon and allspice in a large bowl.
3. Combine zucchini and the rest of ingredients until well combined.
4. Pour the batter evenly into a greased 9" 9" pan.
5. Bake for 20 minutes or until wooden toothpick inserted in center comes out clean.
6. Let cool and serve.

I'll take a slice!

- 6 oz. all-purpose white flour
- 1/2 c. packed brown sugar
- 1 tsp. low-sodium baking powder
- 1 tsp. ground cinnamon
- 1/4 tsp. ground allspice
- 2/3 c. shredded zucchini
- 1 c. blueberries
- 3 tbsp. canola oil
- 2 tbsp. unsalted butter, melted
- 2 tbsp. low-fat milk
- 1 tsp. vanilla extract
- 1 egg, lightly beaten
- cooking spray

Percent Daily Values (DV) are based on a 2000 calorie diet

Calories	199.8	Protein	3.4g
Total Fats	7.1g	Potassium	215.5mg
Sodium	121.9mg	Phosphorus	7.1%

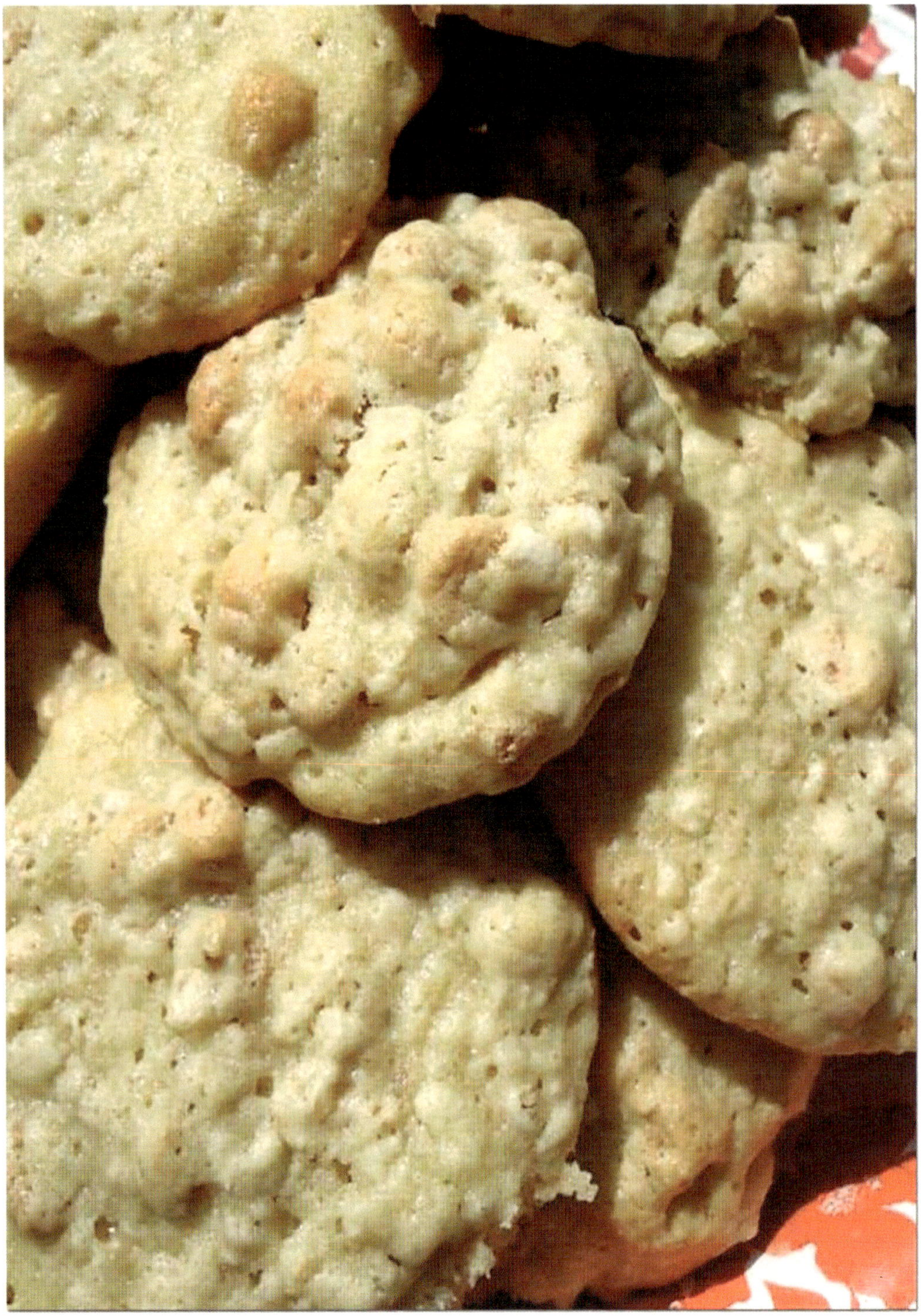

Cowboy Cookies

Serves: 24
Prep Time: 15 min.
Cooking Time: 10 min.

1. Preheat oven to 350°F.
2. In a large bowl, beat sugar and butter on medium speed until blended.
3. Beat in the egg, oil, and vanilla.
4. Stir in flour, oats, baking soda and cereal.
5. Drop dough by tablespoons onto an ungreased cookie sheet.
6. Bake 9-10 minutes or until light brown.
7. Cool on a wire rack.

YeeHaw!

1 1/2 c. sugar
1/4 c. unsalted butter, softened
1/2 c. fat-free egg substitute
1/3 c. canola oil
1 tsp. vanilla extract
1 1/2 c. all-purpose flour
1 c. quick-cooking oats
1 tsp. baking soda
3 c. Cheerios cereal

Percent Daily Values (DV) are based on a 2000 calorie diet

Calories	144.1	Protein	2.1g
Total	5.4g	Potassium	32.1mg
Sodium	82.3mg	Phosphorus	1.3%

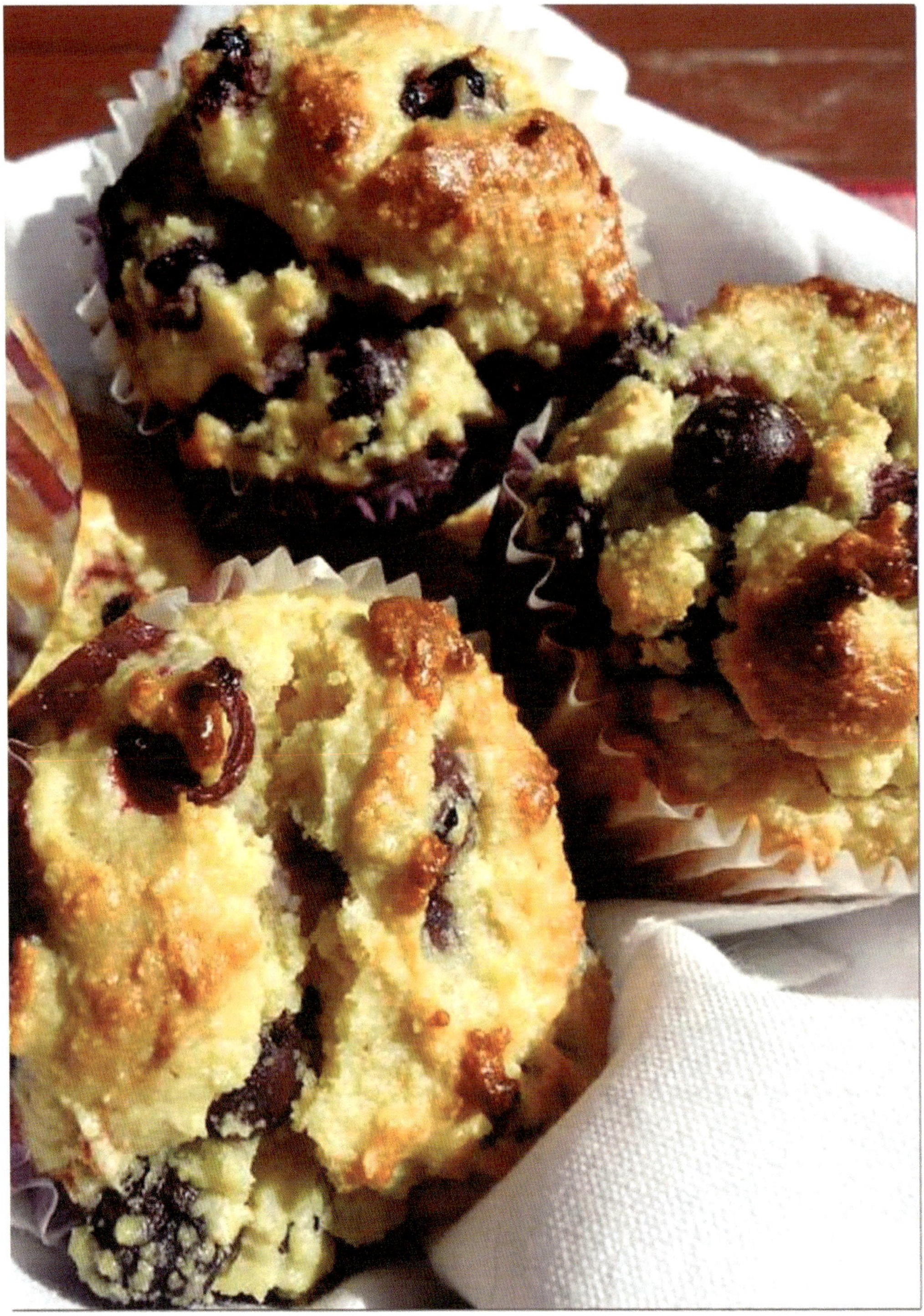

California Chai Cupcakes

Serves: 20
Prep Time: 30 min.
Cooking Time: 20 min.

1. Preheat oven to 350°F.	1/2 c. unsalted butter
2. Line a muffin tin with paper baking cups.	2 eggs
3. In a medium bowl, stir together flour, chai spice, cream of tartar and baking soda.	2 c. all-purpose flour
	1 tbsp. Chai spice seasoning
4. Set aside.	1 tsp. baking soda
5. In a large mixing bowl, beat butter and sugar on medium speed until light and fluffy.	3/4 tsp. cream of tartar
	1 1/2 c. sugar
6. Add the eggs and vanilla, beat well.	1/2 tsp. vanilla extract
7. Slowly add the flour mixture and buttermilk beating on low speed just until combined.	1 1/4 c. low-fat buttermilk
	3/4 c. blueberries

8. Stir in the blueberries.
9. Spoon batter into muffin cups filling each about 2/3 full.
10. Bake for 20 minutes or until a wooden toothpick inserted in center comes out clean.
11. Let cool completely on wire racks.

So scrumptious!

Percent Daily Values (DV) are based on a 2000 calorie diet

Calories	162.7	Protein	2.7g
Total	5.5g	Potassium	65.3mg
Sodium	88.4mg	Phosphorus	4.1%

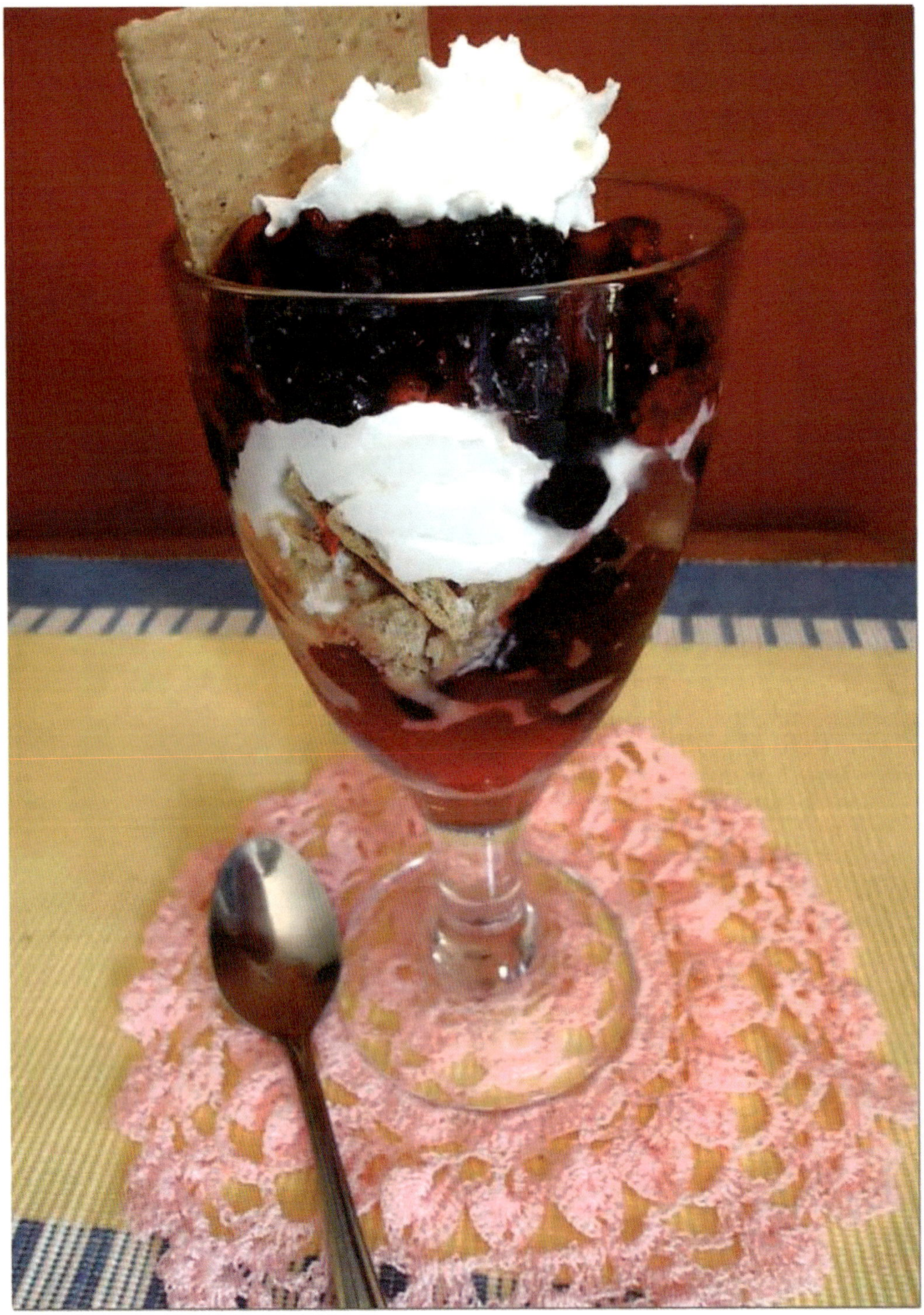

Red, White, and Blue Parfait

Serves: 4
Prep Time: 10 min.
Cooking Time: -

1. Make the jello according to package directions.
2. Refrigerate jello until set.
3. In parfait glass, layer jello, graham crackers, and whipped cream until 2/3 full.
4. Top with blueberries and whipped cream.
5. Serve with a graham cracker on the side.

Great for 4th of July!

1 - 14 oz. box red jello
1 pint blueberries
4 graham crackers, crushed
1 container non-dairy whipped cream

Percent Daily Values (DV) are based on a 2000 calorie diet

Calories	150.6	Protein	2.0g
Total	0.5g	Potassium	84.5mg
Sodium	109.3mg	Phosphorus	2.2%

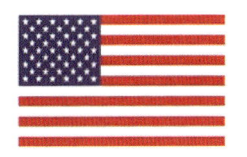

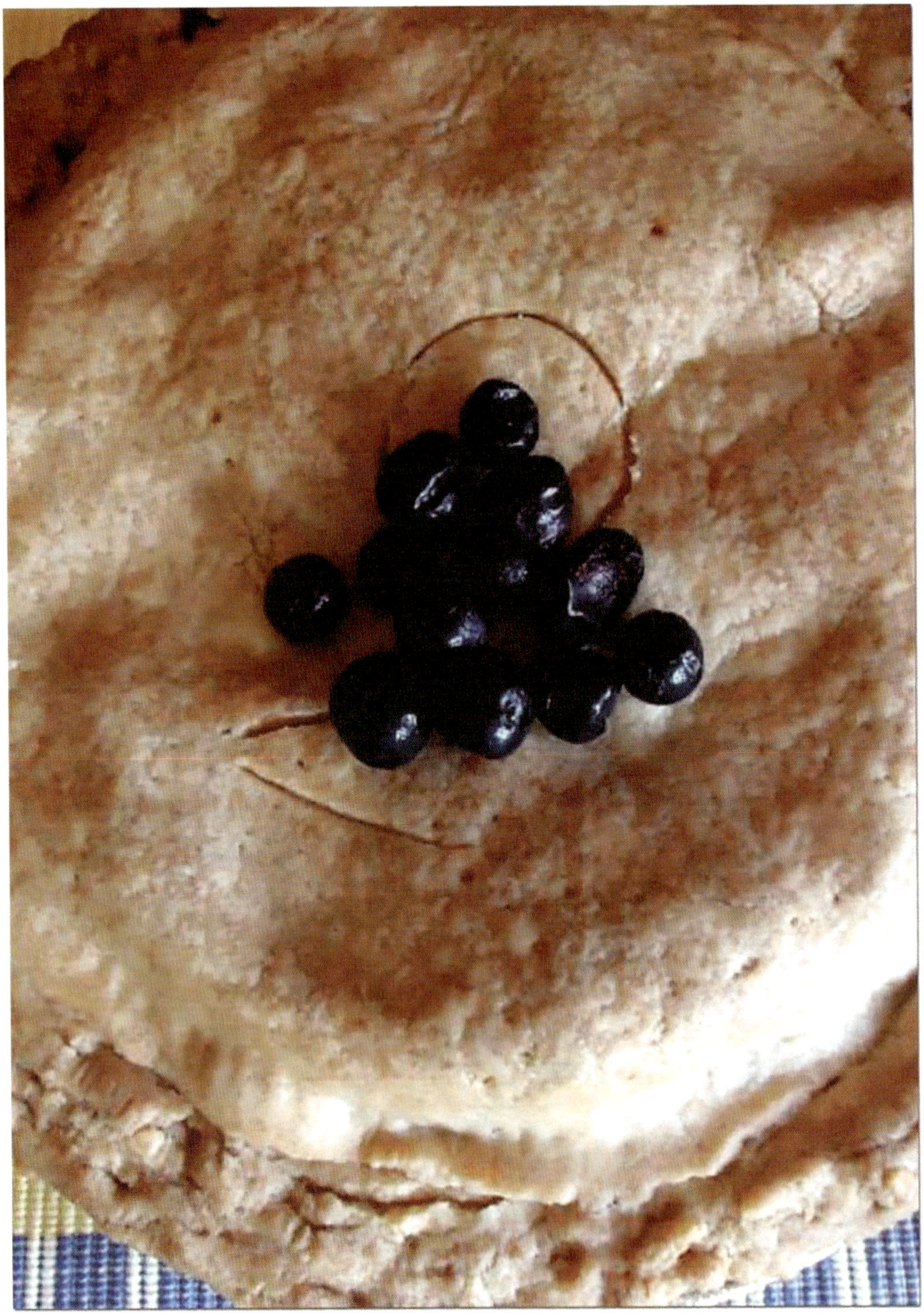

All-American Blueberry Pie

Serves: 8
Prep Time: 10 min.
Cooking Time: 50 min.

1. Simmer 3 cups blueberries with maple syrup for 20 minutes.
2. When done, pour into a bowl and stir in the rest of the blueberries.
3. Add in the tapioca, lemon juice, and nutmeg.
4. Let cool.
5. Preheat the oven to 375 F.
6. Line a pie pan with one of the prepared pie crusts.
7. Pour the blueberry mixture into pan and dot with the butter.
8. Place the second pie crust on top and crimp the edges.
9. Take a knife and slice an X in center of top pie crust.
10. Bake until golden brown, about 30 minutes.
11. Let cool before slicing.

- 6 c. blueberries
- 1/4 c. maple syrup
- 3 tbsp. quick-cooking tapioca
- 4 tbsp. unsalted butter
- 1 tbsp. lemon juice
- 1/4 tsp. nutmeg
- 1 box prepared pie crusts

Percent Daily Values (DV) are based on a 2000 calorie diet

Calories	277.7	Protein	0.8g
Total	4.1g	Potassium	99.7mg
Sodium	127.8mg	Phosphorus	1.2%

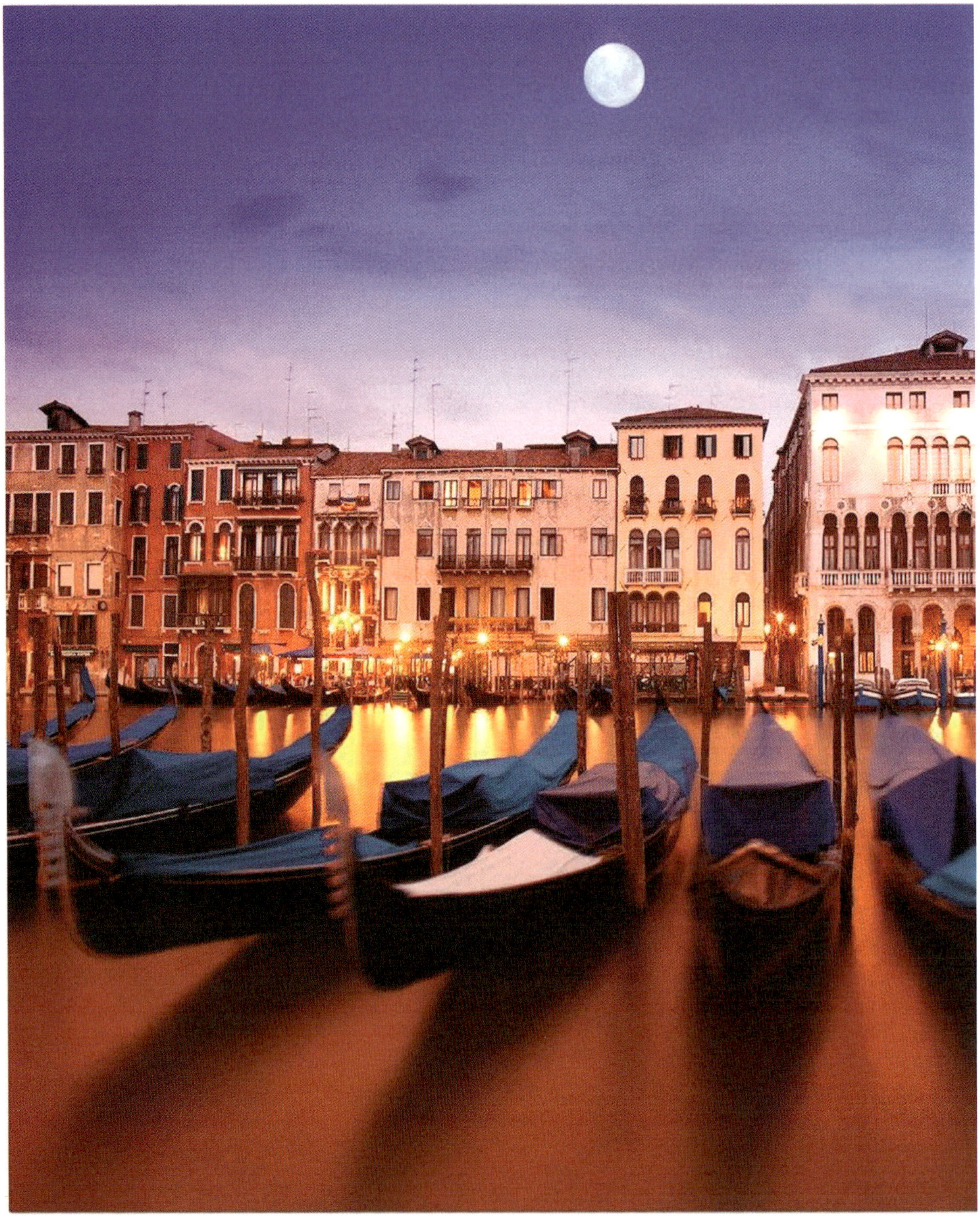

Italy

The Culinary history of Italy is deeply indebted to the geographical and cultural differences of the people. An emphasis on good, healthy living made up of well-prepared food is the center of the Italian gastronomic cultural tradition today.

61 | Strawberry Caprese Salad

63 | Asparagus Risotto

65 | Italian Stuffed Red Bell Peppers

67 | Lemon-Parsley Pesto

69 | Mediterranean Stuffed Shells

71 | Pollo alla Griglia e Squash

73 | Insalata di Pasta di Granchio

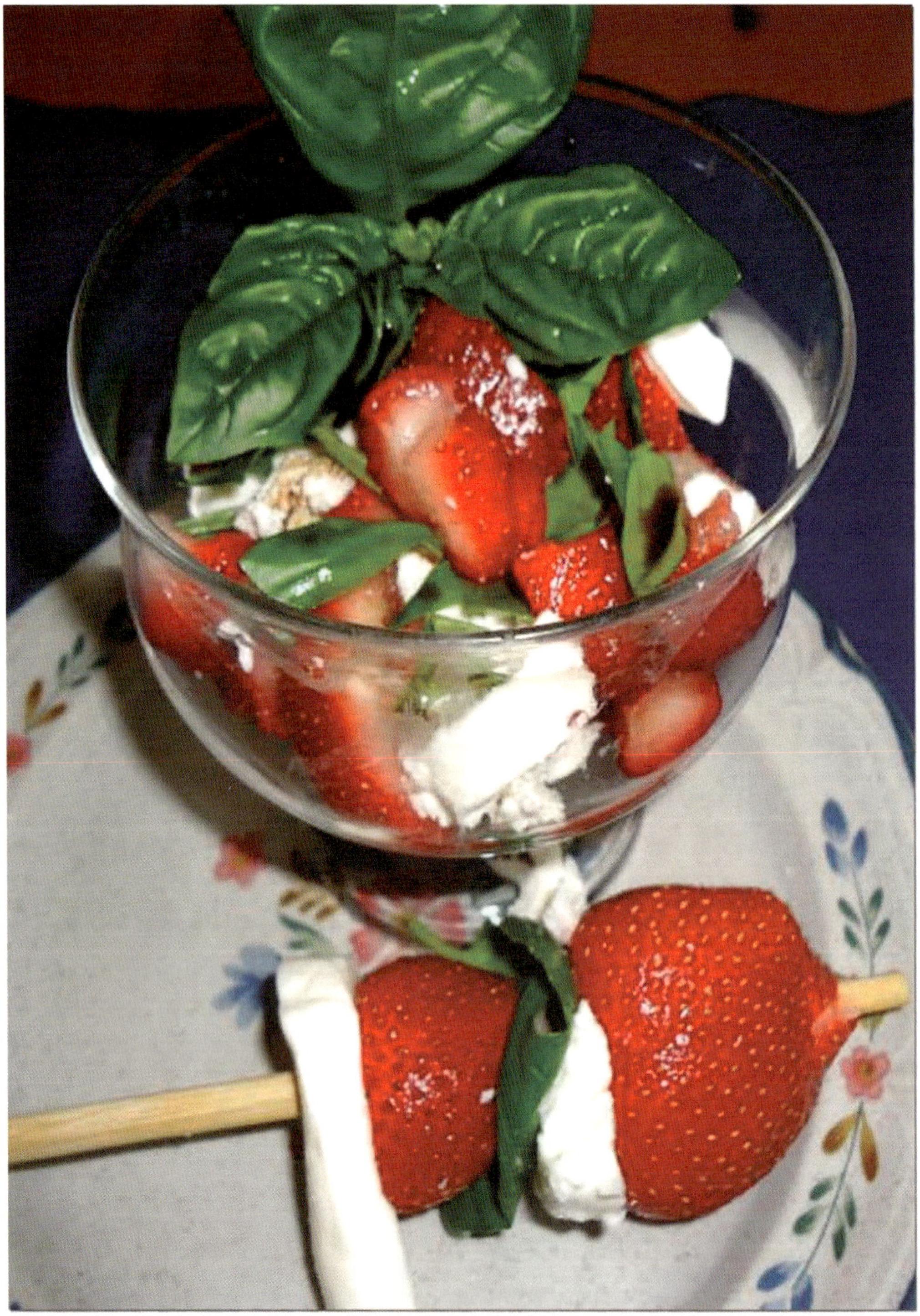

Strawberry Caprese Salad

Serves: 2
Prep Time: 10 min.
Cooking Time: -

1. In a large bowl, combine all the ingredients and mix gently.
2. Serve skewered or in a bowl for a delicous appetizer.

Piatto estivo scrumptious!

2 c. strawberries, hulled, sliced
1 c. fresh mozzarella, sliced
2 tbsp. balsamic vinegar
1 handful basil leaves, julienned

Percent Daily Values (DV) are based on a 2000 calorie diet

Calories	169.5	Protein	7.7g
Total Fats	6.7g	Potassium	362.4g
Sodium	247.7mg	Phosphorus	3.4%

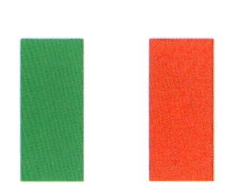

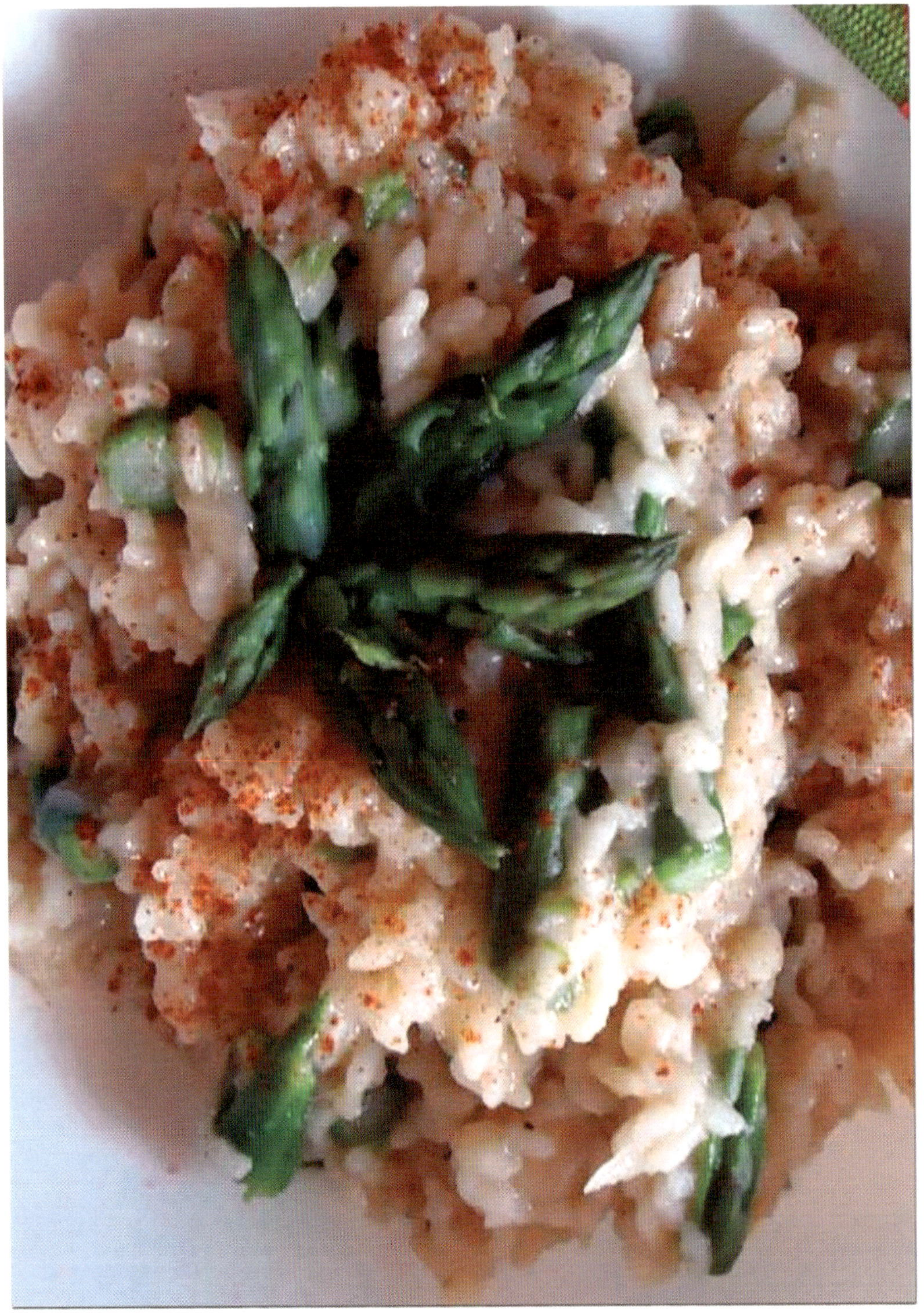

Asparagus Risotto

Serves: 4
Prep Time: 10 min.
Cooking Time: 30 min.

1. Cook the asparagus in boiling water until it turns dark green, about 3 minutes. Set aside.
2. In a large saucepan, melt the butter.
3. Add the onion and sauté until tender.
4. Add the garlic and sauté 1 minute more.
5. Add the rice and stir to coat with the butter.
6. Add the wine, and stir while simmering until the wine has cooked off.
7. Add 1/2 c. of the stock at a time and stir while simmering.
8. Continue until the rice is cooked, about 20 minutes.
9. Stir in the cheese and remaining butter.
10. Remove from heat and mix in asparagus and lemon juice.
11. Garnish with paprika if desired.

2 c. asparagus trimmed, cut into 1" pieces
1 tbsp. unsalted butter
1 medium yellow onion, diced
1 clove garlic, chopped
1 c. arborio rice
1/2 c. dry white wine
2 c. no-sodium vegetable broth
2 tbsp. parmigiano reggiano, grated
1 tbsp. unsalted butter
1 tsp. lemon juice
pepper to taste

A true taste of Italy!

Percent Daily Values (DV) are based on a 2000 calorie diet

Calories	244.2	Protein	5.8g
Total Fats	2.9g	Potassium	252.8g
Sodium	170.1mg	Phosphorus	7.4%

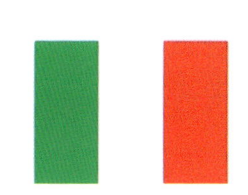

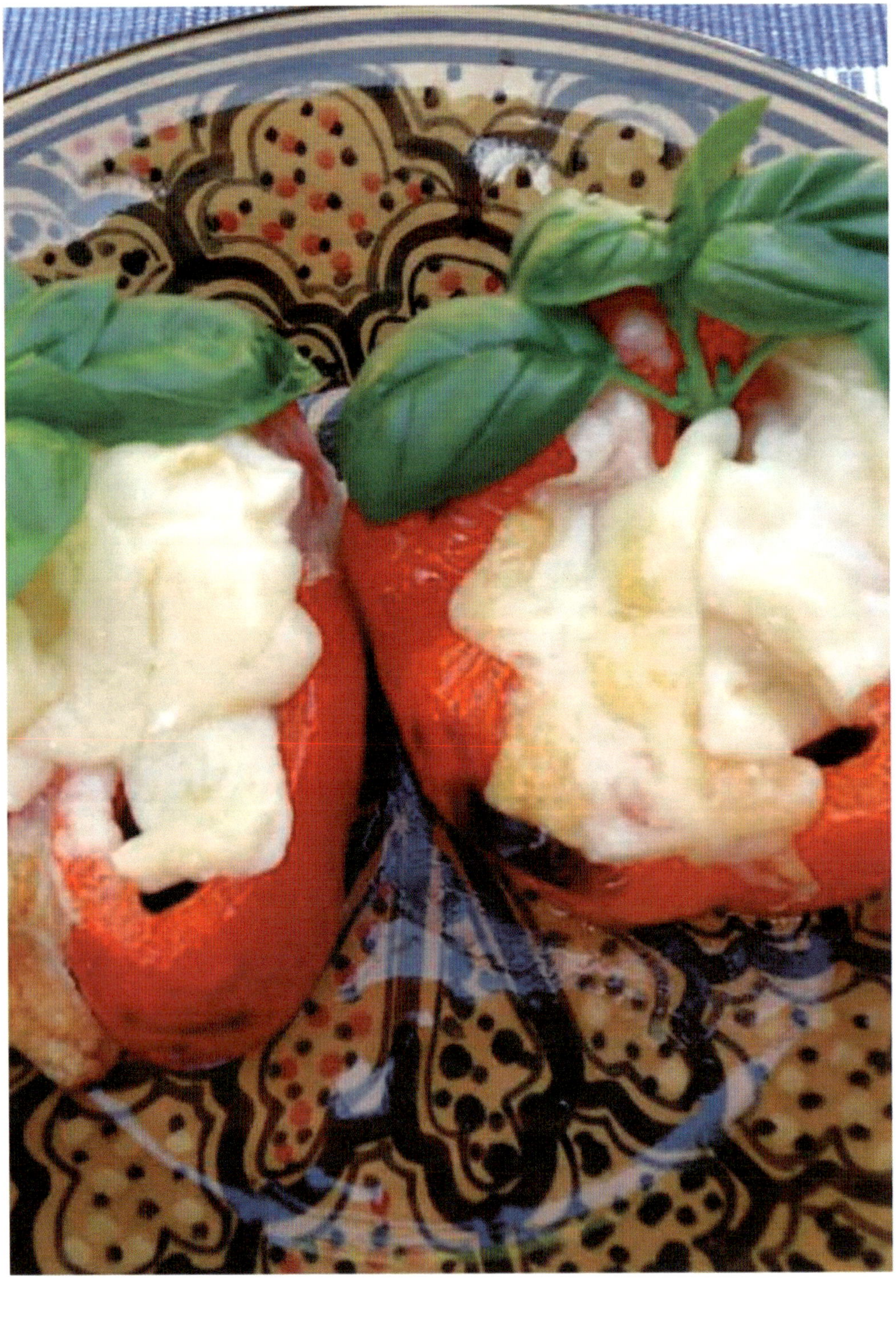

Italian Stuffed Red Bell Peppers

Serves: 4
Prep Time: 10 min.
Cooking Time: 30 min.

1. Preheat oven to 350°F.
2. In a large stockpot, par-boil peppers for 5 minutes.
3. Drain, and cool. Set aside.
4. In skillet, brown the ground beef and drain excess fat.
5. Add onion and garlic, cook for an additional 2 minutes.
6. Add the roasted peppers, basil, and seasonings.
7. Add the rice and simmer for 10 minutes.
8. If needed add a little water.
9. Stuff the peppers with mixure and bake for 15 minutes.
10. Remove from oven, and place a slice of cheese on top of each pepper.
11. Return to oven and bake for 5 minutes longer.

4 red bell peppers, washed, cored
1/2 lb. lean ground beef
1/2 c. cooked long grain white rice
1 medium onion, chopped fine
1 clove garlic, chopped fine
1/4 c. roasted red peppers, chopped
1 bunch fresh basil, chopped
1 tbsp. Italian seasoning
4 slices mozzarella cheese
Pepper to taste

Mama Mia!

Percent Daily Values (DV) are based on a 2000 calorie diet

Calories	260.4	Protein	15.6g
Total Fats	10.1g	Potassium	207.2g
Sodium	171.6mg	Phosphorus	9.7%

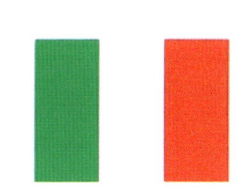

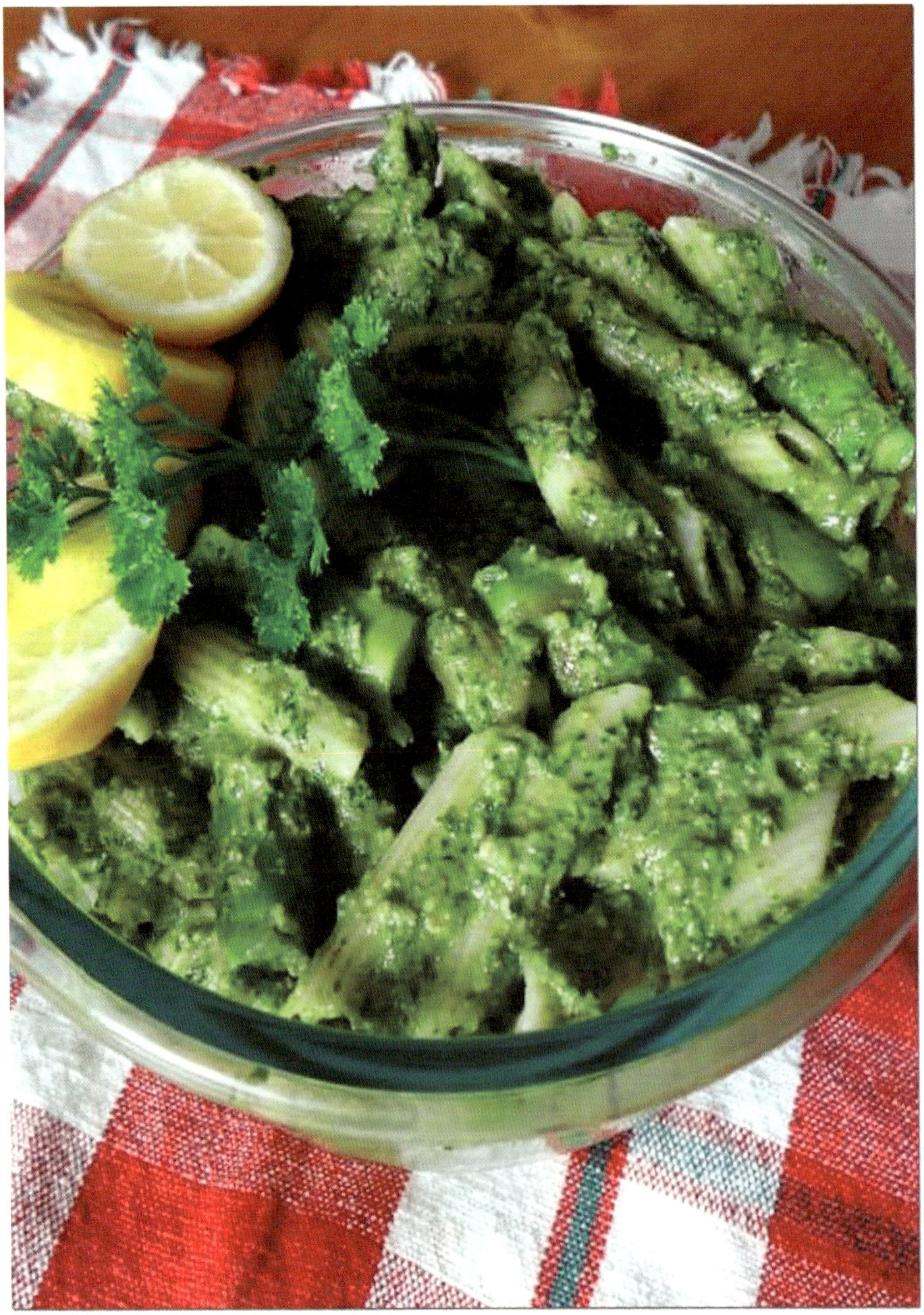

Lemon-Parsley Pesto

Serves: 4
Prep Time: 10 min.
Cooking Time: 30 min.

1. In a food processor, put all the ingredients in and whizz until a paste has formed.
2. Serve with penne or your choice of pasta.

Buon appetito!

- 1 bunch parsley
- 1 garlic clove, peeled
- 1/4 c. breadcrumbs
- 2 tbsp. lemon juice
- 2/3 c. olive oil
- 1 tsp. lemon zest
- black pepper to taste

Percent Daily Values (DV) are based on a 2000 calorie diet

Calories	168.0	Protein	0.3g
Total Fats	18.1g	Potassium	23.1g
Sodium	11.2mg	Phosphorus	0.04%

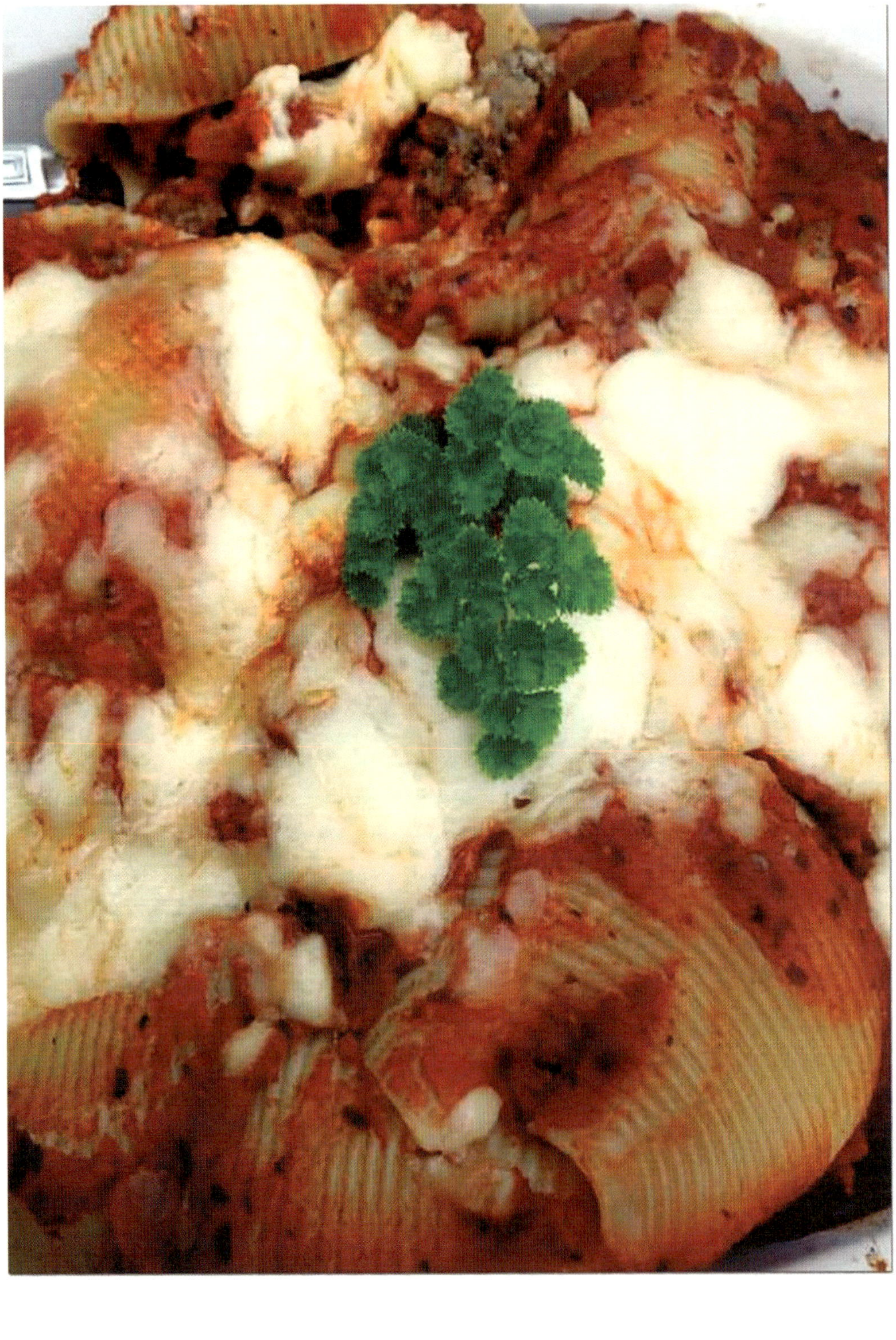

Mediterranean Stuffed Shells

Serves: 8
Prep Time: 20 min.
Cooking Time: 25 min.

1. Preheat oven to 350°F.
2. In a large skillet, brown the beef, onion and garlic. Drain and let cool.
3. Stir in the cheese, crumbs, parsley and egg.
4. Cook the shells according to package directions.
5. Drain and rinse with cold water.
6. For the sauce, blend all the ingredients together until smooth.
7. Take the cooked shells, and stuff them with the cooked meat mixture.
8. In a 9" x 12" casserole dish, spoon half of the sauce over the bottom.
9. Place the stuffed shells on top of the sauce, and pour the remaining sauce over the shells.
10. Sprinkle with the parmesan cheese, cover and bake for 25 minutes or until bubbly.

1 lb. extra-lean ground beef
1 large onion, chopped
1 clove garlic, minced
1/2 c. light mozzarella, shredded
1/2 c. Italian breadcrumbs
1/4 c. parsley, chopped
1 egg, beaten
1/4 c. parmesan, grated
1 large box giant pasta shells

Red Pepper Sauce:
7 oz. jar roasted red peppers, drained
1 garlic clove, chopped
1/2 c. light mayonnaise
1 tsp. fresh lemon juice
pepper to taste

Ne voglio ancora!

Percent Daily Values (DV) are based on a 2000 calorie diet

Calories	268.6	Protein	10.3g
Total Fats	3.7g	Potassium	35.9g
Sodium	301.1mg	Phosphorus	6.1%

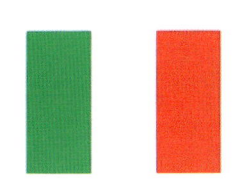

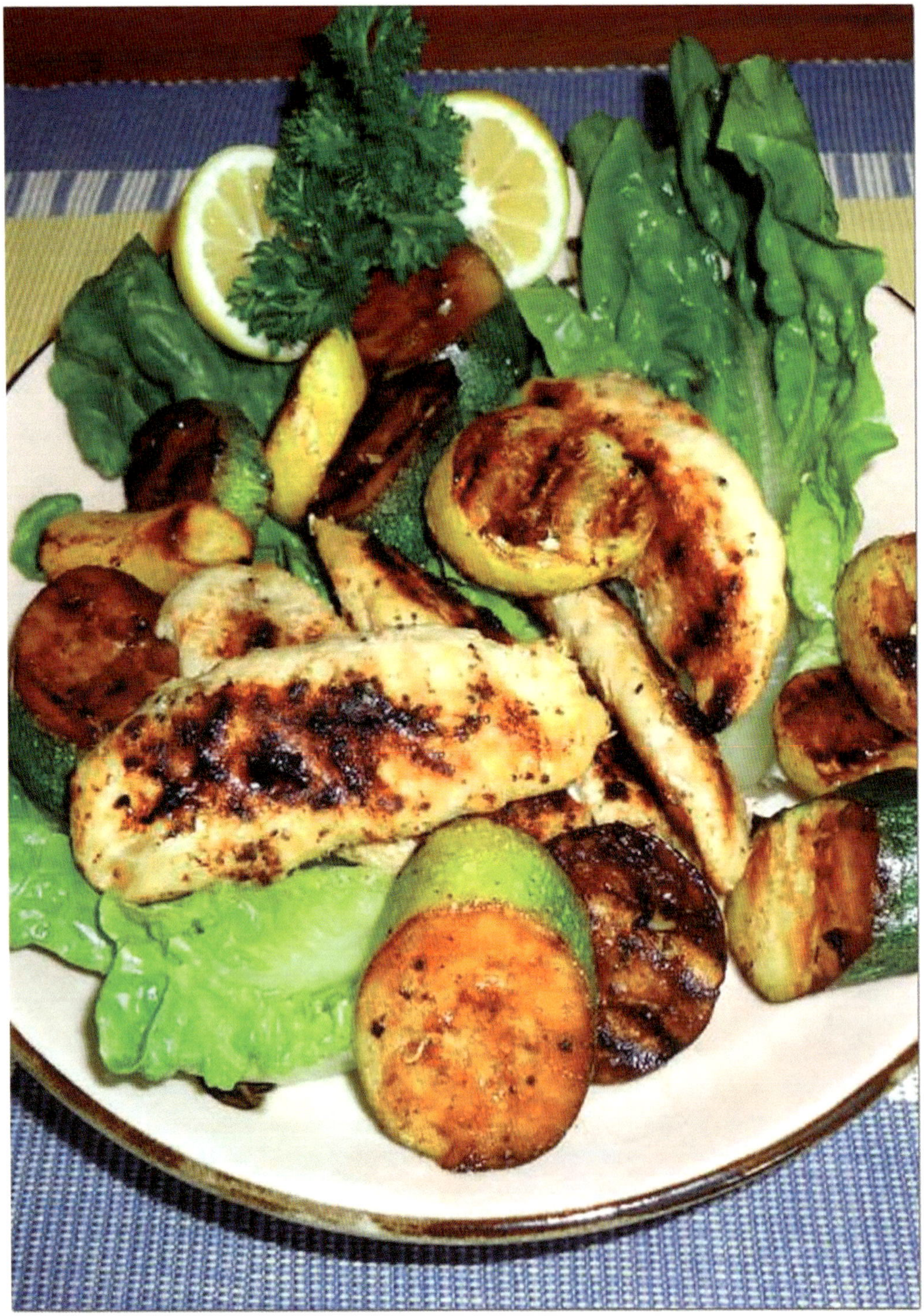

Pollo alla griglia e Squash

Serves: 8
Prep Time: 15 min.
Cooking Time: 20 min.

1. In a large freezer bag or sealable container, place all the ingredients (except for romaine lettuce) and mix well.
2. Let marinade in the refrigerator for 2 hours or overnight.
3. In a large grill pan, cook the chicken and veggie mixture until golden brown, stirring frequently.
4. Serve on top of the romaine lettuce leaves.

1 lb. chicken tenders
2 zucchini, sliced
2 summer squash, sliced
3 tbsp. extra-virgin olive oil
2 fresh rosemary sprigs
2 tbsp. garlic, minced
2 lemons, quartered
2 tsp. ground pepper
dash hot sauce
baby romaine leaves

Complimenti alla cuoca!

Percent Daily Values (DV) are based on a 2000 calorie diet

Calories	110.2	Protein	13.0g
Total Fats	3.2g	Potassium	118.0g
Sodium	24.1mg	Phosphorus	1.8%

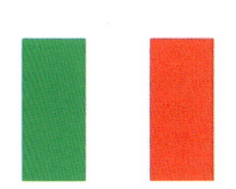

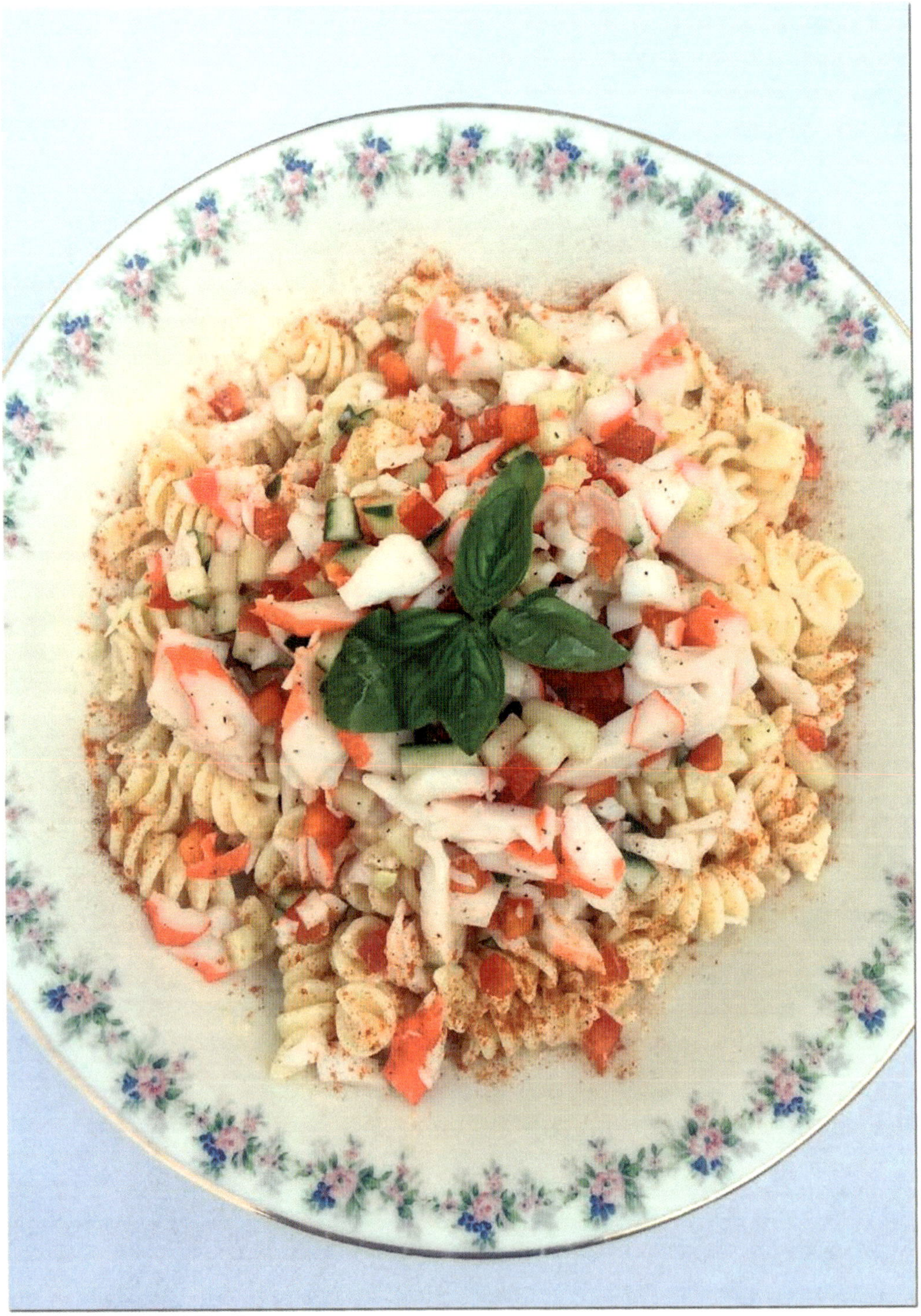

Insalata di Pasta di Granchio

Serves: 8
Prep Time: 20 min.
Cooking Time: 10 min.

1. Cook the pasta in a large pot of boiling water according to package instructions.
2. Drain and rinse with cold water.
3. In a small bowl, combine the yogurt, red pepper, celery, horseradish, paprika and mustard.
4. In a large bowl, combine the pasta, crabmeat, cucumber, celery, lemon juice and pepper.
5. Mix the pasta with the dressing and transfer to a serving dish.
6. Garnish with the fresh basil.

Fresco e croccante!

- 12 oz. rotelle pasta
- 1 red bell pepper, seeded, chopped
- 1 c. crabmeat, picked through for shells, chopped
- 1/2 cucumber, seeded, chopped
- 1 tbsp. lemon juice
- 1 c. low-fat yogurt
- 2 celery stalks, chopped
- 2 tsp. creamed horseradish
- 1/2 tsp. Dijon mustard
- 1/2 tsp. paprika
- black pepper
- fresh basil to garnish

Percent Daily Values (DV) are based on a 2000 calorie diet

Calories	166.2	Protein	9.6g
Total Fats	1.1g	Potassium	188.0g
Sodium	98.0mg	Phosphorus	9.5%

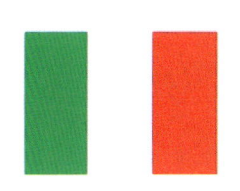

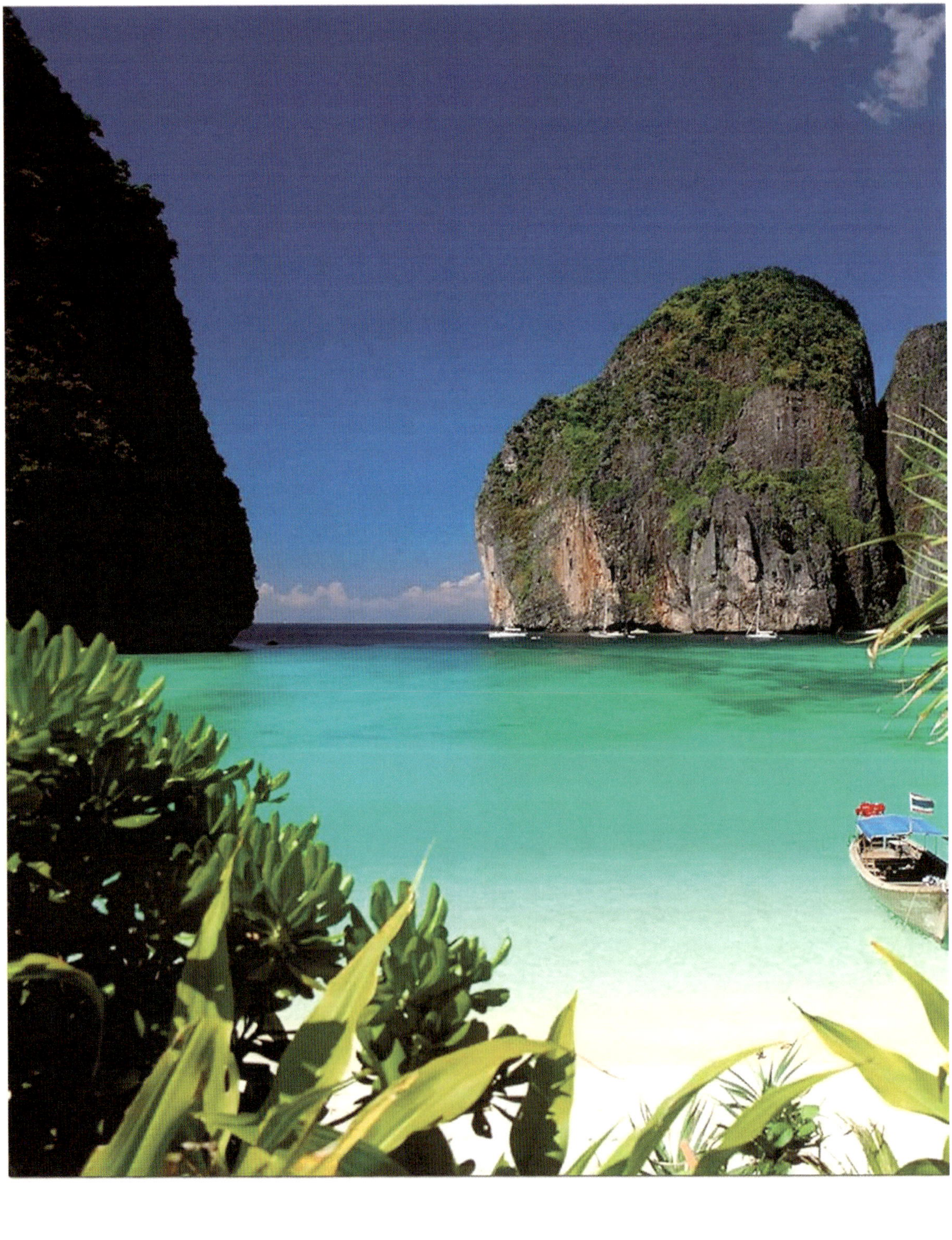

Spain

Endless cultures that have settled or passed through Spain have influenced the Spanish cuisine. For instance, rice came from the Moors, olive oil from the Greeks, and tomatoes, vanilla and chocolate came from America.

77 | Camarones y Pimienta Tortilla

79 | Spanish Chorizo Breakfast Pizza

81 | Melocoton con Atun

83 | Spanish Ham Croquettes

85 | Chicken Couscous Salad

87 | Spanish Orzo and Shrimp

89 | Pastel de Carne

91 | Arroz con Leche

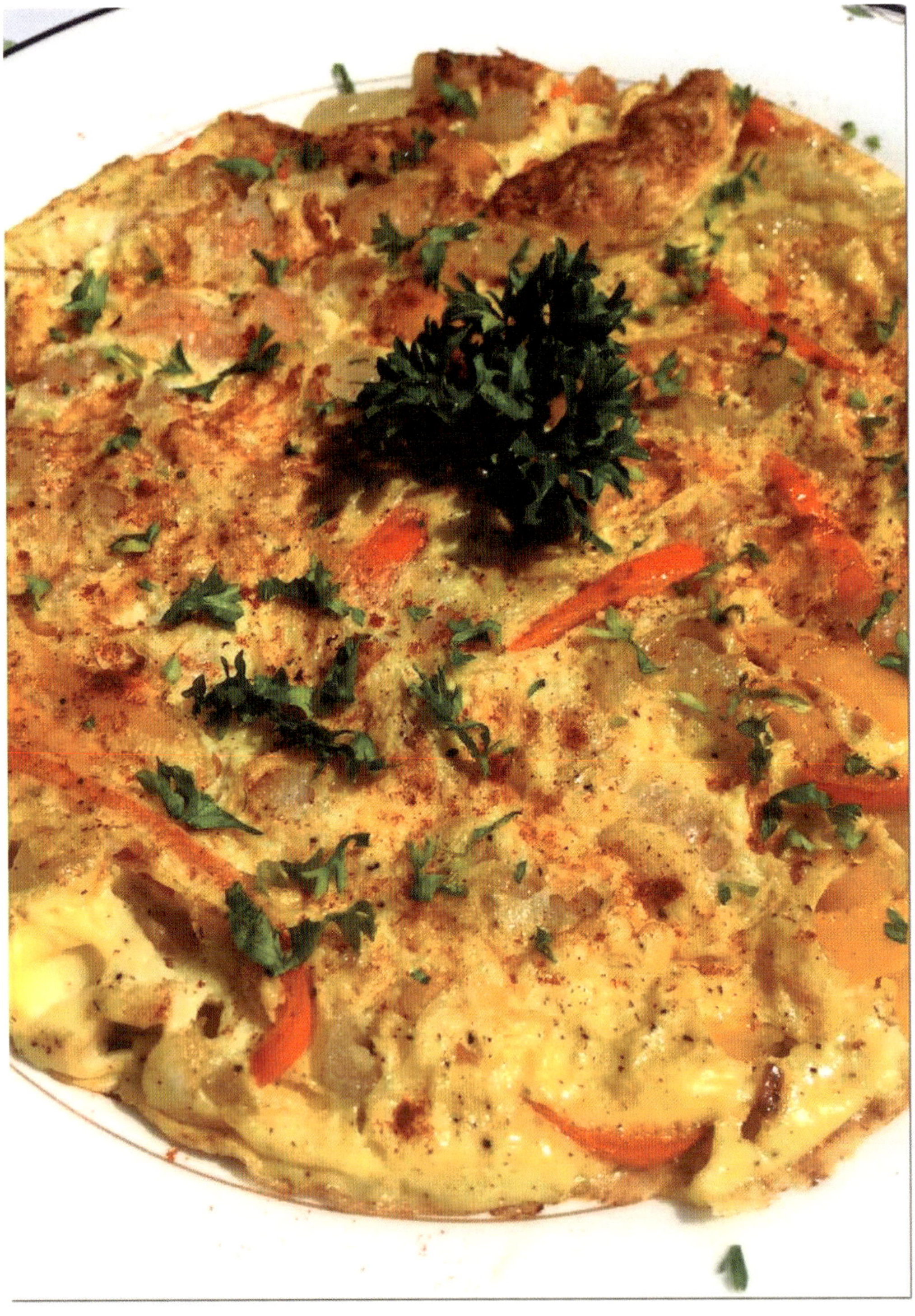

Camarones y Pimienta Tortilla

Serves: 8
Prep Time: 15 min.
Cooking Time: 15-20 min.

1. Peel and devein the shrimp if needed and season with pepper.
2. Cut the peppers into thin strips.
3. In a bowl, beat the eggs and season with pepper.
3. In a large skillet, spray cooking spray and sauté the shrimp for 1 minute and set aside.
4. Add the garlic, onion and peppers, and cook over low heat for 5-6 minutes until tender.
5. Add the shrimp and cook for 2 minutes more.
6. Pour the eggs over the shrimp mixture and cook over low heat for 4-5 minutes.
7. Flip and cook for an additional 4 minutes.
8. Remove and place on a plate and garnish with chopped parsley if desired.

9 oz. shrimp
ground pepper
1/2 onion, chopped
1 small red pepper
1 small orange pepper
1 small yellow pepper
2 cloves garlic, minced
4 eggs
cooking spray
parsley for garnish

Percent Daily Values (DV) are based on a 2000 calorie diet

Calories	92.3	Protein	10.6g
Total Fats	4.0g	Potassium	120.6g
Sodium	124.9mg	Phosphorus	10.1%

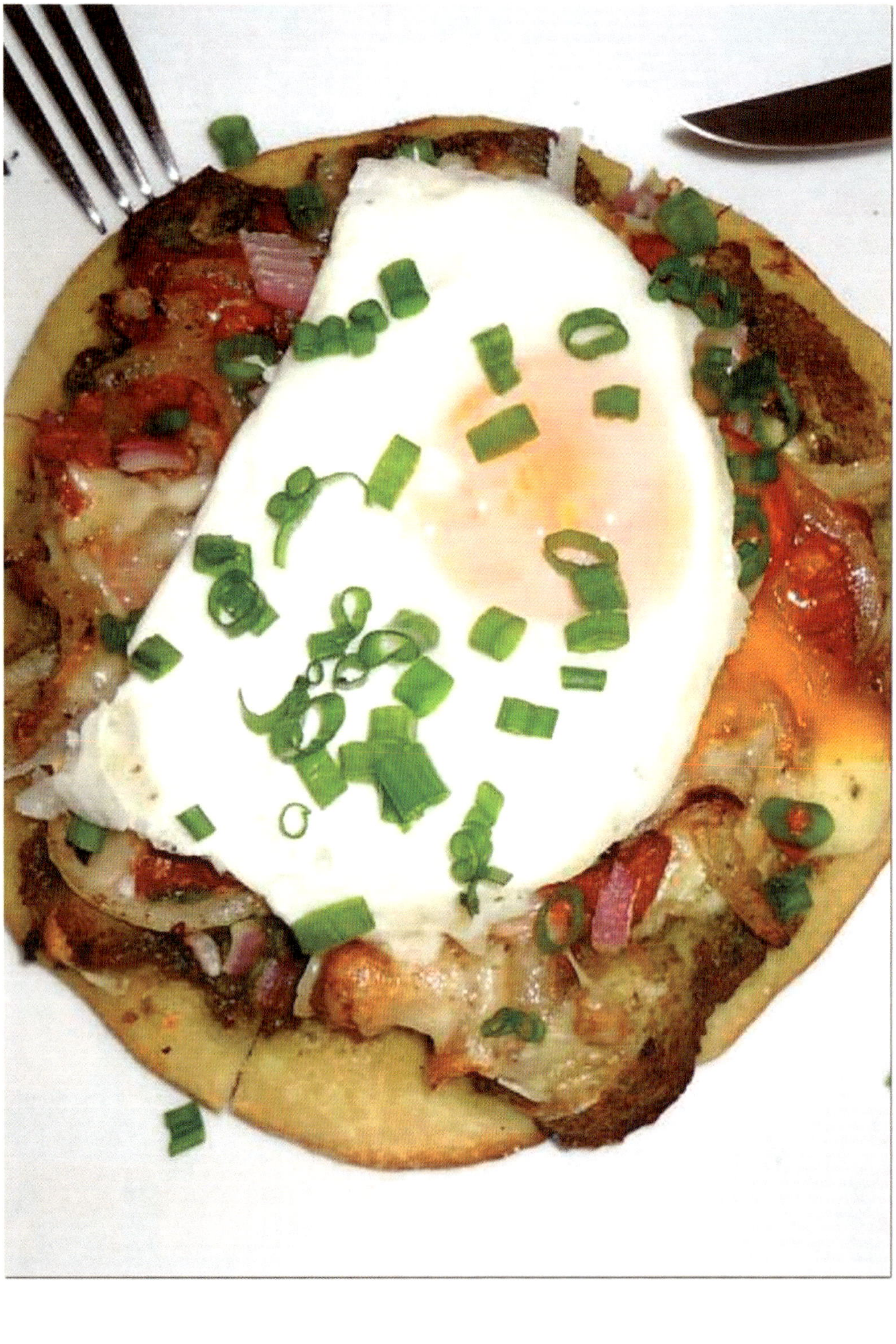

Spanish Chorizo Breakfast Pizza

Serves: 4
Prep Time: 20 min.
Cooking Time: 10 min.

1. Preheat oven to 400 F.
2. In a small bowl, mix together onions, garlic, oregano and pepper. Set aside.
3. Brush the flatbread with the pesto, and then spread the onion mixture on top.
4. Sprinkle with the chorizo and provolone cheese.
5. Bake the pizza for 10 minutes, or until the cheese is lightly browned.
6. Meanwhile, heat a skillet over medium heat, add the oil.
7. Carefully break the eggs into the skillet and cook until the whites are set.
8. When pizza is done, slice into quarters, and place a fried egg on top of each slice.
9. Sprinkle the sliced scallion on top for a beautiful garnish.

4 oz. vegan chorizo, crumbled
1 small red onion, sliced
1 large light flatbread
1/2 shredded provolone cheese
1/2 c. lemon-pesto (pg. 67)
1 tbsp. olive oil
4 small eggs
1 tbsp. oregano
1 clove garlic, minced
black pepper to taste
sliced scallions for garnish

Tengo mucha hambre!

Percent Daily Values (DV) are based on a 2000 calorie diet

Calories	252.3	Protein	12.8g
Total Fats	10.4g	Potassium	85.8g
Sodium	264.6mg	Phosphorus	13.6%

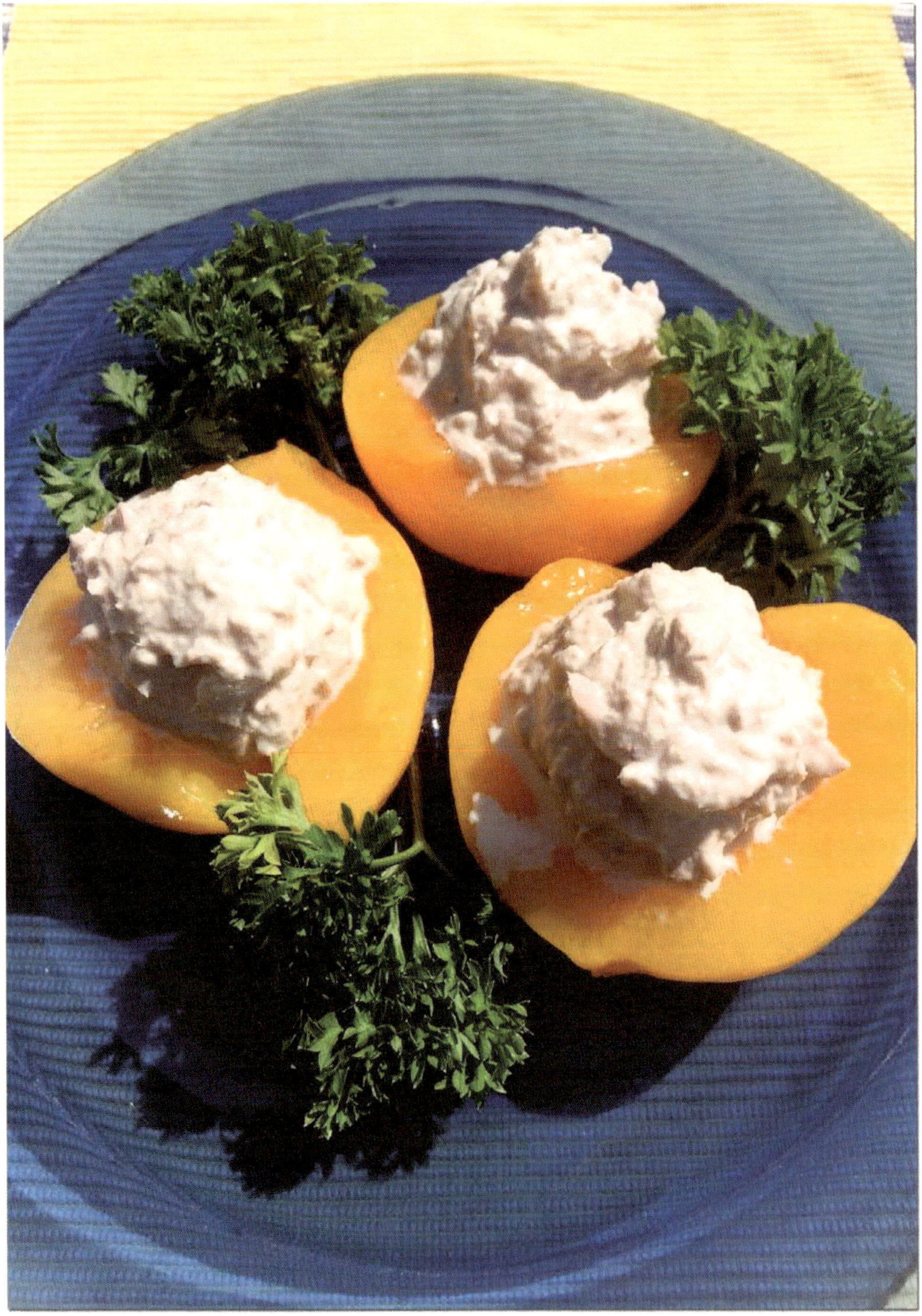

Melocoton Con Atun

Serves: 4
Prep Time: 5 min.
Cooking Time: -

1. Open the peaches and tuna, drain both.
2. In a small bowl, flake the tuna and add the mayonnaise, mix well.
3. Arrange the peach halves on a serving platter cut side up.
4. Spoon the tuna into the center of each peach and serve!

1 can peach halves, in light syrup
1 can tuna, in water
1 tbsp. light mayonnaise

Percent Daily Values (DV) are based on a 2000 calorie diet

Calories	95.5	Protein	8.5g
Total Fats	1.4g	Potassium	160.6g
Sodium	130.3mg	Phosphorus	8.1%

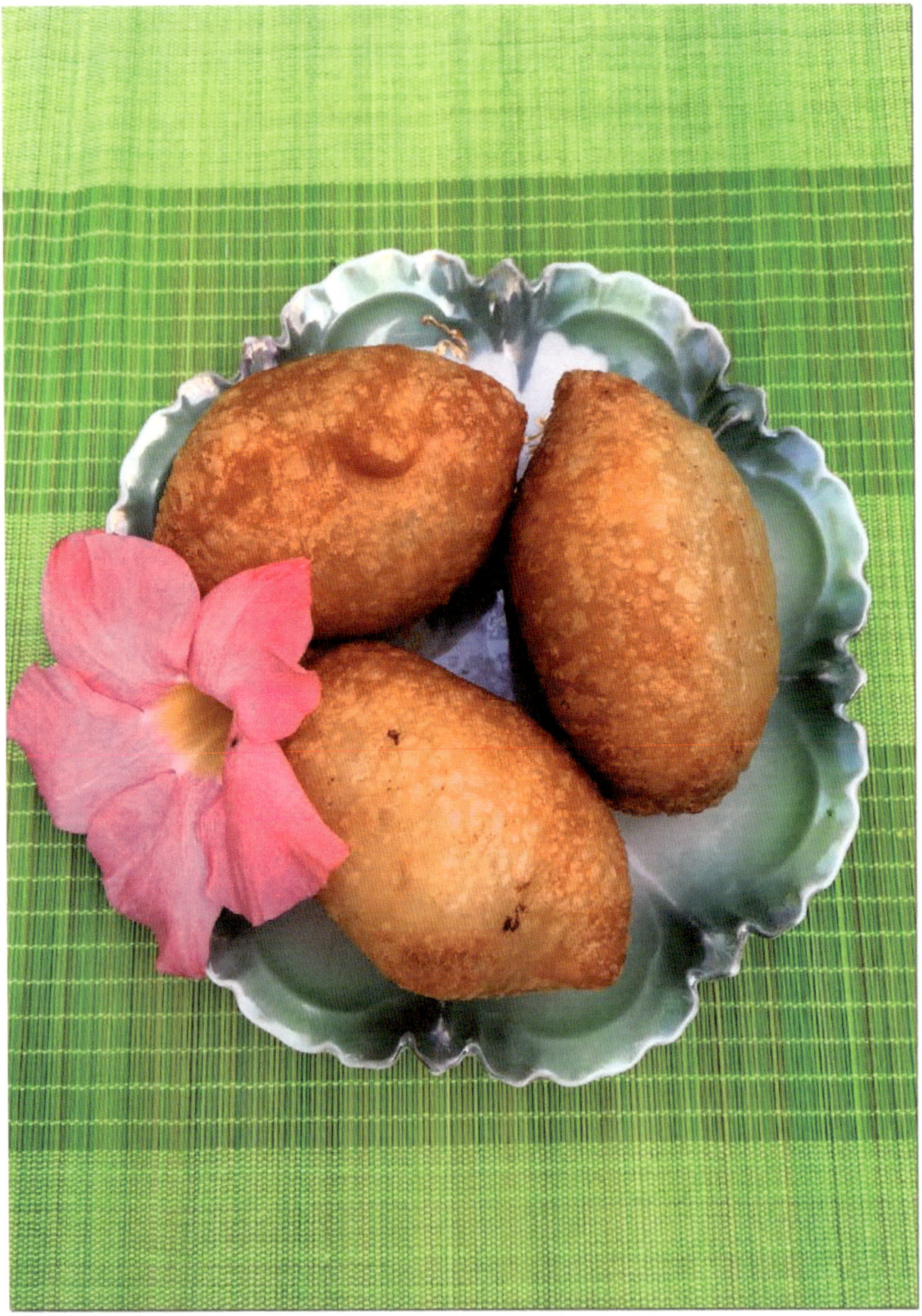

Spanish Ham Croquettes

Serves: 6
Prep Time: 10 min.
Cooking Time: 25 min.

1. In a small saucepan over medium heat, heat the olive oil.
2. Add the flour and cook for 3 minutes stirring constantly.
3. Gradually add the almond milk and the chicken broth stirring without stopping.
4. Add the nutmeg and pepper and cook until the sauce is thick and smooth, stirring constantly.
5. Add the minced ham, reduce the heat to low and cook for 2 minutes stirring constantly.
6. Remove from heat and allow to cool.
7. Refrigerate for 3 hours.
8. Meanwhile pour the breadcrumbs into a small wide bowl.
9. Place the egg and water mixture in another bowl.
10. Remove the dough from the refrigerator and divide the mixture into 1" balls and set on a plate.
11. In a large skillet, add enough olive oil to coat the pan to 1/2" deep.
12. Heat the olive oil to 355°F. and dip the croquettes in the egg first and then coat with the breadcrumbs.
13. Place the croquettes in the hot oil, frying quickly, turning several times until golden brown in color.
14. Remove with a slotted spoon and set on a paper towel. Serve immediately.

1/2 c. fat-free sodium-free chicken broth

6 tbsp. extra-light olive oil

3/4 c. flour

1 1/2 c. almond milk

1/2 tsp. nutmeg

ground black pepper

1/2 c. extra-lean ham, finely minced

2 eggs, lightly beaten w/ 2 tsp. water

1/2 c. plain breadcrumbs

canola oil for frying

Percent Daily Values (DV) are based on a 2000 calorie diet

Calories	234.7	Protein	6.0g
Total Fats	12.1g	Potassium	111.4g
Sodium	201.3mg	Phosphorus	6.1%

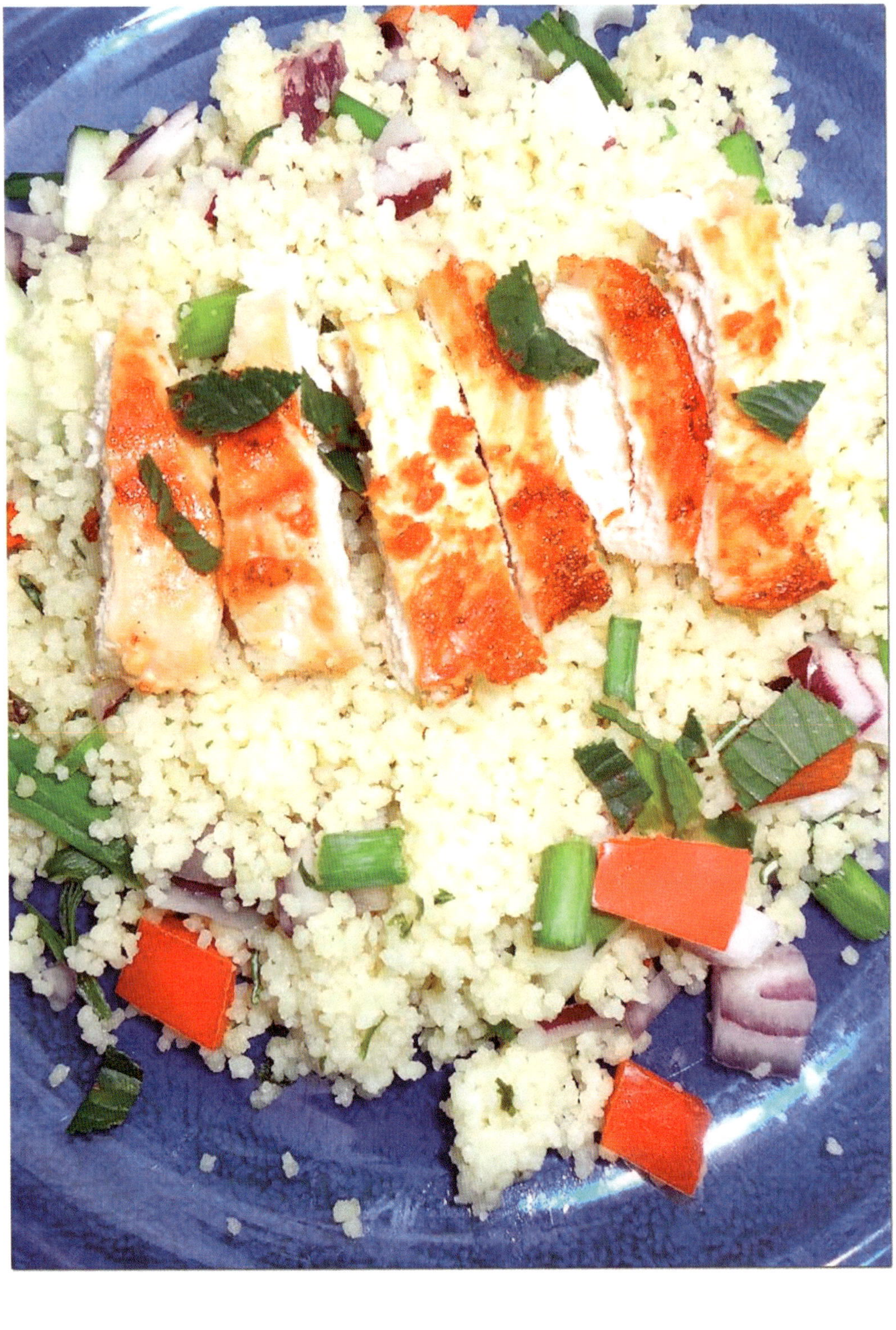

Chicken and Couscous Salad

Serves: 10
Prep Time: 10 min.
Cooking Time: 15 min.

1. Season chicken on both sides with pepper, garlic and rosemary.
2. Drizzle both sides with lemon juice and 1 tsp. olive oil.
3. Refrigerate 20 minutes.
4. Preheat a grill pan on medium-high heat, and spray with cooking spray.
5. Arrange the chicken on the grill and cook until firm, about 5 minutes per side.
6. Transfer the chicken to a cutting board and slice into 1" pieces.
7. In a large bowl, add the couscous, onions, cucumber, peppers, mint and zest.
8. Squeeze the lemon juice over everything and drizzle with the remaining olive oil.
9. Plate salad and serve with the grilled chicken on top.

250g couscous, cooked
6 skinless chicken cutlets, sliced thin
ground black pepper
1 clove garlic, minced
1 tbsp. fresh rosemary, chopped
juice of 1 lemon
1 tsp. extra-virgin olive oil
3/4 c. water
zest of 1 lemon
juice of 1 lemon
cooking spray
1 tbsp. extra-virgin olive oil
2 c. cucumber, peeled, diced
1 red pepper, quartered
2 spring onions, sliced
sprig of mint, chopped

Percent Daily Values (DV) are based on a 2000 calorie diet

Calories	108.5	Protein	11.1g
Total Fats	3.2g	Potassium	140.2g
Sodium	27.2mg	Phosphorus	9.3%

85 | SPAIN

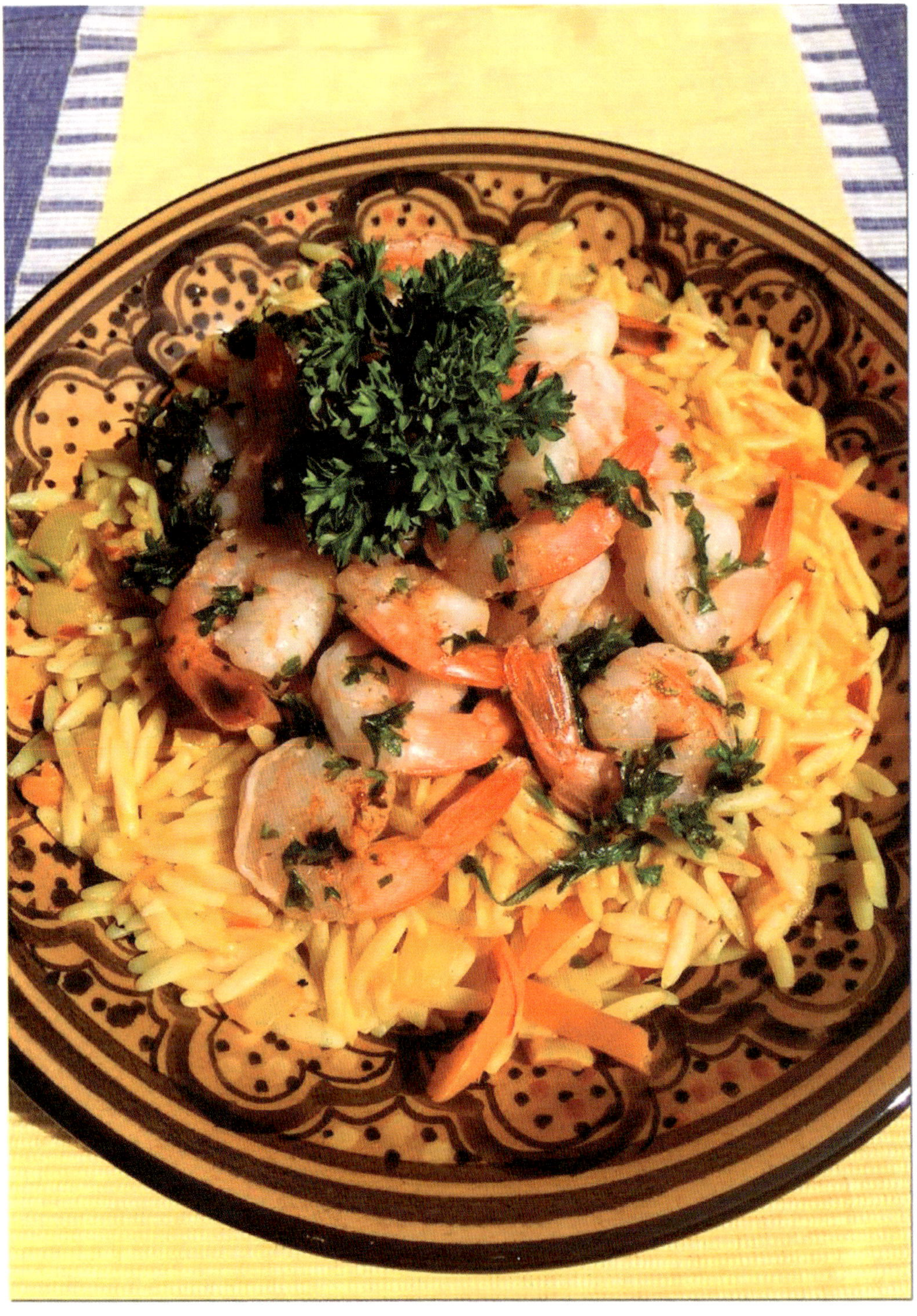

Spanish Orzo and Shrimp

Serves: 8
Prep Time: 20 min.
Cooking Time: 20 min.

1. Cook the orzo according to package directions.
2. Drain and cover.
3. While pasta is cooking, in a small saucepan, steep the saffron in the chicken broth over low heat.
4. In a large skillet, spray with cooking spray, and over medium heat, cook the onion, peppers, garlic and turmeric. Cook for 5 minutes stirring frequently.
5. Remove the vegetables to a large bowl, add the olive oil to the hot skillet and add the shrimp, cook for 3 minutes or until no longer pink.
6. Add the parsley, paprika and lemon juice to the shrimp and toss well.
7. Add the saffron broth and orzo to the vegetables and toss well.
8. To serve, plate the orzo mixture and top with shrimp.

1/2 lb. orzo pasta
2 pinches saffron threads
1 c. low-sodium fat-free chicken broth
cooking spray
1 tsp. olive oil
1 onion, chopped
1 small roasted red pepper, chopped
1 small yellow pepper, chopped
1 small orange pepper, chopped
2 cloves garlic, chopped
1 tsp. ground turmeric
1 lb. medium shrimp, shelled, deveined
1/4 c. parsley, chopped
1 tsp. paprika
juice of 1 lemon

Percent Daily Values (DV) are based on a 2000 calorie diet

Calories	150.5	Protein	12.1g
Total Fats	1.0g	Potassium	126.3g
Sodium	154.1mg	Phosphorus	8.6%

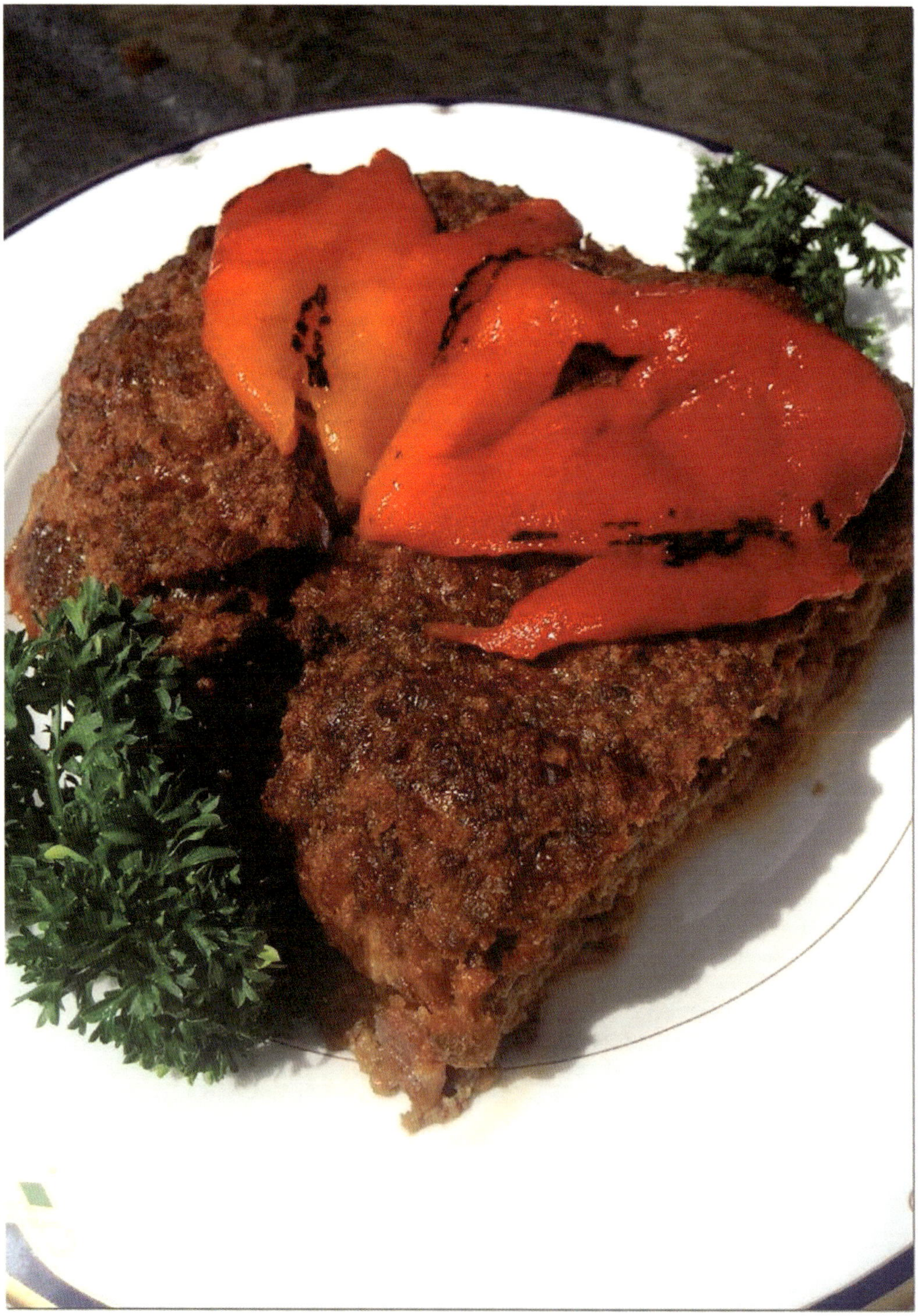

Pastel de Carne

Serves: 12
Prep Time: 10 min.
Cooking Time: 45 min.

1. Preheat the oven to 350°F.
2. In a large bowl, beat the egg.
3. Mix in all the ingredients.
4. Spray a loaf pan with cooking spray and pack in the meat mixture.
5. Bake uncovered in oven for 1 hour.
6. Top with roasted red peppers if desired.

A hearty meal!

16 oz. extra-lean ground beef
1 egg
1 c. rolled oats
1/4 c. onions, chopped
1 tsp. worcestershire sauce
2 tsp. packed brown sugar
1 tsp. yellow mustard
1/2 c. fire-roasted red peppers, chopped fine
black pepper to taste
cooking spray

Percent Daily Values (DV) are based on a 2000 calorie diet

Calories	96.1	Protein	9.6g
Total Fats	3.7g	Potassium	15.6g
Sodium	61.1mg	Phosphorus	1.2%

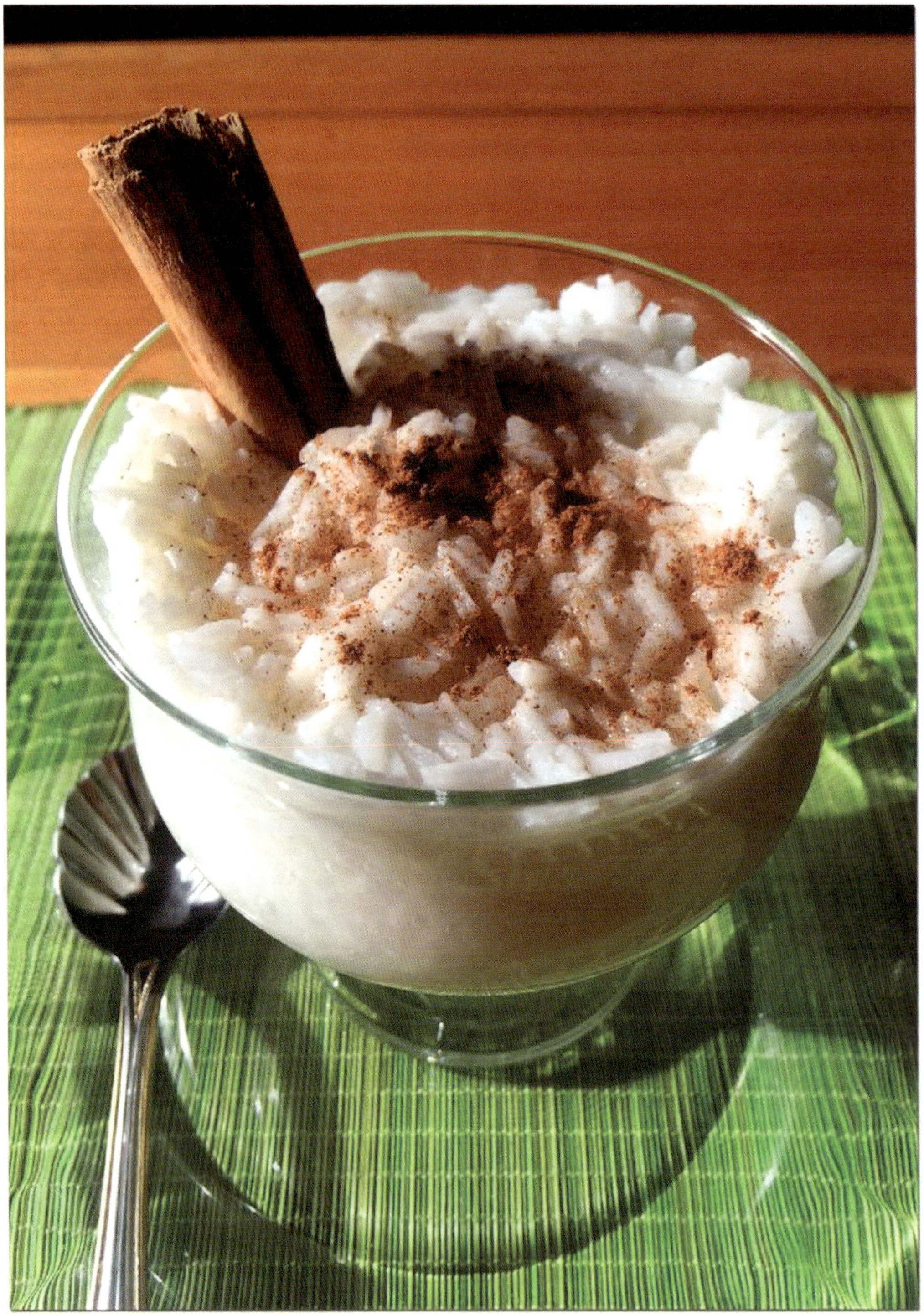

Arroz con Leche

Serves: 6
Prep Time: 15 min.
Cooking Time: 40 min.

1. In a large pot, boil 3 c. water and add the rice.
2. Reduce the heat to simmer. Cover and cook for 10 minutes.
3. Turn off the burner and allow rice to sit.
4. Pour the milk into another large pot and add the sugar.
5. Turn the burner on low and stir until the sugar is dissolved.
6. Bring the almond milk to a boil over medium heat.
7. Add the drained rice, margarine, cinnamon stick and lemon zest to milk.
8. Boil mixture again for 15 minutes.
7. Remove from heat and pour into a serving dish.
8. Let cool for 15 minutes before serving, top with ground cinnamon.

2 c. almond milk
1 1/2 c. medium-grain rice
1/2 c. granulated sugar
1/2 stick unsalted margarine
1 tsp. lemon zest
1 cinnamon stick
2 tsp. ground cinnamon

Percent Daily Values (DV) are based on a 2000 calorie diet

Calories	201.7	Protein	1.5g
Total Fats	7.4g	Potassium	77.8g
Sodium	98.3mg	Phosphorus	2.5%

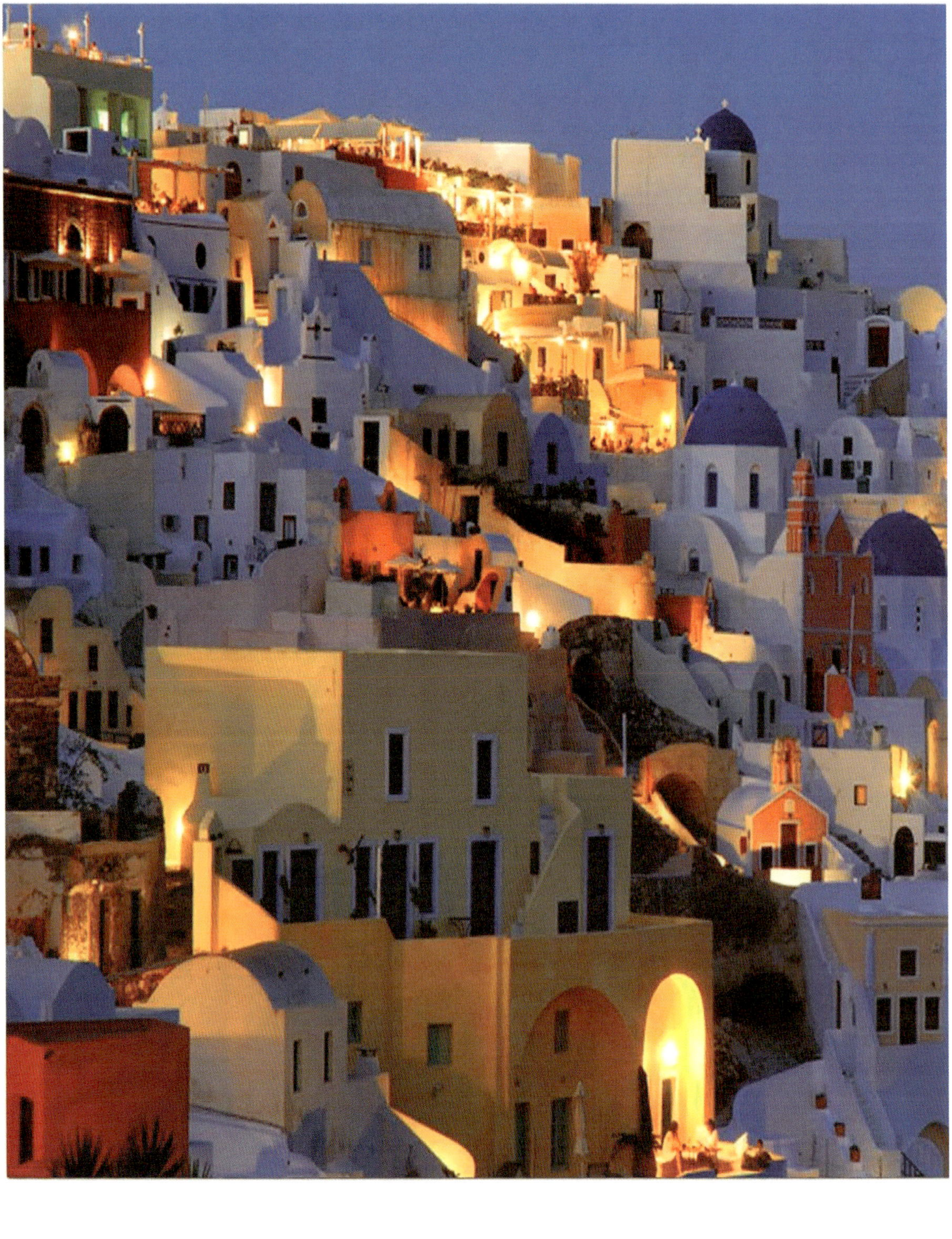

Greece

Follow a trip back through Greece's history and enjoy a diverse array of incredible foods. Greece's climate is perfect for growing lemon and olive trees which are emphasized in Greek cuisine. Seafood is also a mainstay of the diet as 20% of Greece is made up of islands.

95 | Greek Lemon Mint Soup

97 | Grilled Lemon Planks with Salmon

99 | Greek Cesar Salad

101 | Chicken Pita Burgers

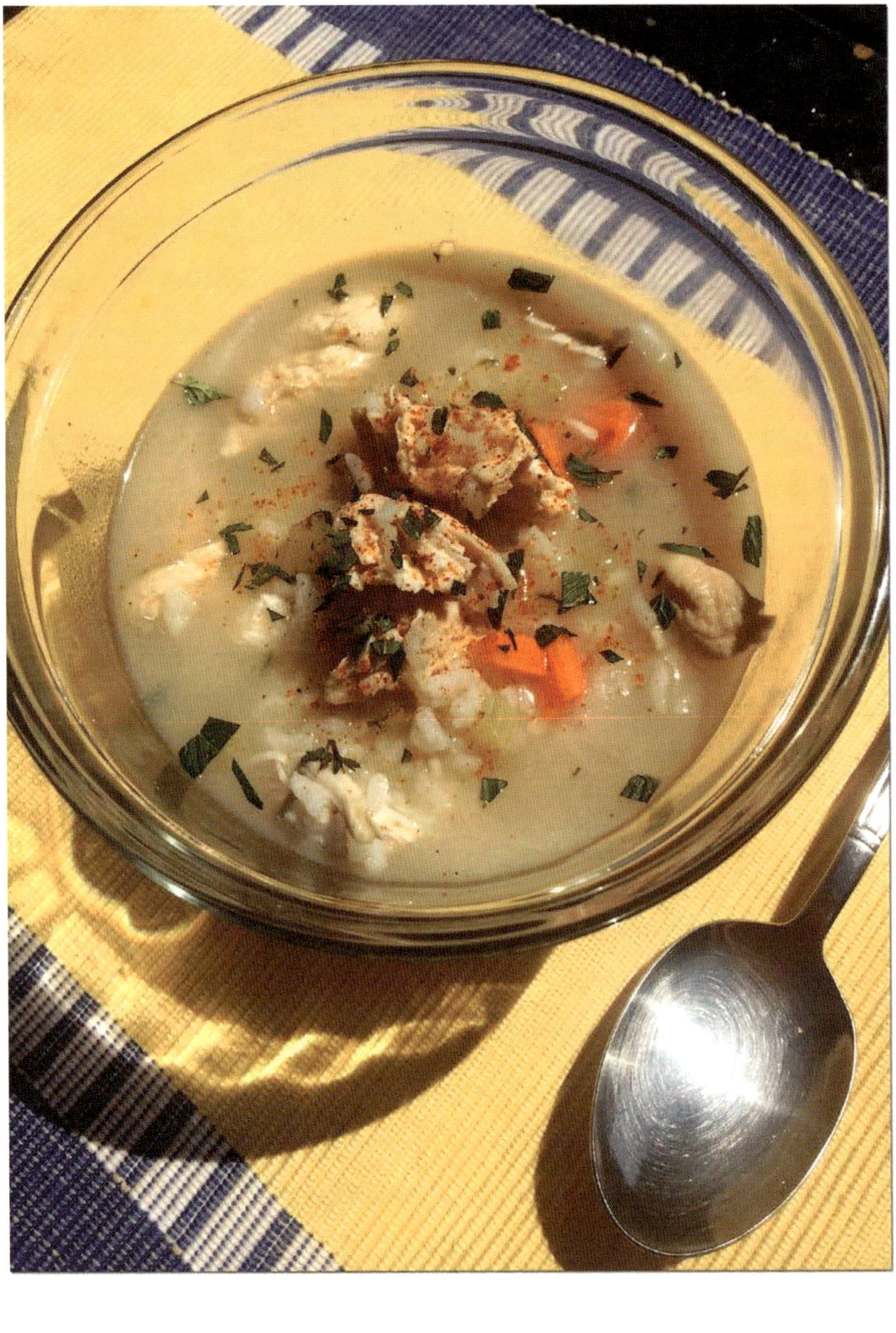

Greek Lemon Mint Soup

Serves: 12
Prep Time: 20 min.
Cooking Time: 1 hr. 35 min.

1. In a large stockpot, combine the chicken, carrots, celery, onion, parsley, mint sprigs, lemon zest, garlic, and red pepper flakes.
2. Add the broth to the pot, bring to a boil and skim off any excess foam that comes to the top.
3. Simmer for 45 minutes, or until the chicken and veggies are cooked.
4. Strain the stock into a large bowl and place the chicken and veggies aside, discarding the parsley and mint sprigs.
5. Return the stock to the pot and let simmer over medium-low heat for about 30 minutes or until the stock has reduced and flavors have intensified.
6. Add the uncooked rice to the stock and simmer until tender, about 20 minutes.
7. Once rice is done, add the chicken and veggies back to the stock and add the lemon juice, chopped mint, and cayenne pepper to taste.

4 c. boneless, skinless chicken, cut into pieces
1 c. carrots, peeled, chopped
1 stalk celery, chopped
1 onion, chopped
3 cloves garlic, crushed
4 sprigs parsley
4 mint sprigs, + 1/4 c. chopped
1 tbsp. lemon zest
1/4 tsp. red pepper flakes
4 quarts fat-free, low-sodium chicken broth
1/4 c. white rice
2 tbsp. fresh lemon juice
cayenne pepper

Percent Daily Values (DV) are based on a 2000 calorie diet

Calories	98.2	Protein	10.5g
Total Fats	1.9g	Potassium	133.3g
Sodium	130.6mg	Phosphorus	8.9%

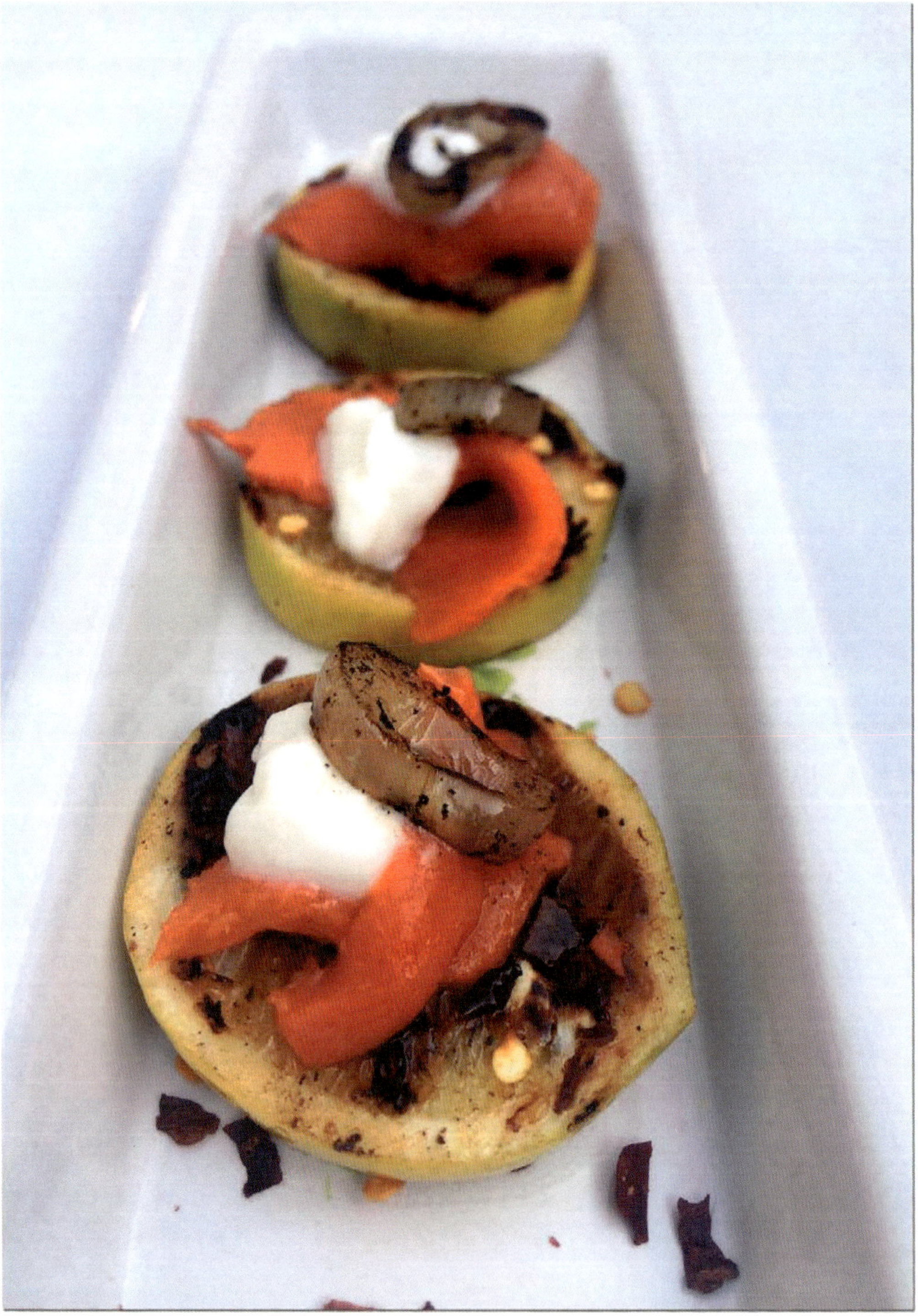

Grilled Lemon Planks w/ Salmon

Serves: 12
Prep Time: 10 min.
Cooking Time: 7 min.

1. Wash the lemons and slice each into three lengthwise sections.
2. Toss the lemons in a small bowl with olive oil and pepper.
3. Heat your grill pan on high heat.
4. Grill the lemons on both sides for 1 minute each side.
5. Transfer to serving platter.
6. Slice the salmon into 2" pieces.
7. Top each lemon with salmon, a dollop of yogurt, grilled shallots and red pepper.

Opa!

3 slices smoked salmon
1/4 c. greek-style plain yogurt
1 tbsp. shallots, cut into rings, grilled
1 tbsp. red pepper flakes
4 lemons
2 tsp. extra-virgin olive oil
black pepper

Percent Daily Values (DV) are based on a 2000 calorie diet

Calories	60.5	Protein	7.8g
Total Fats	2.7g	Potassium	131.2g
Sodium	16.4mg	Phosphorus	8.1%

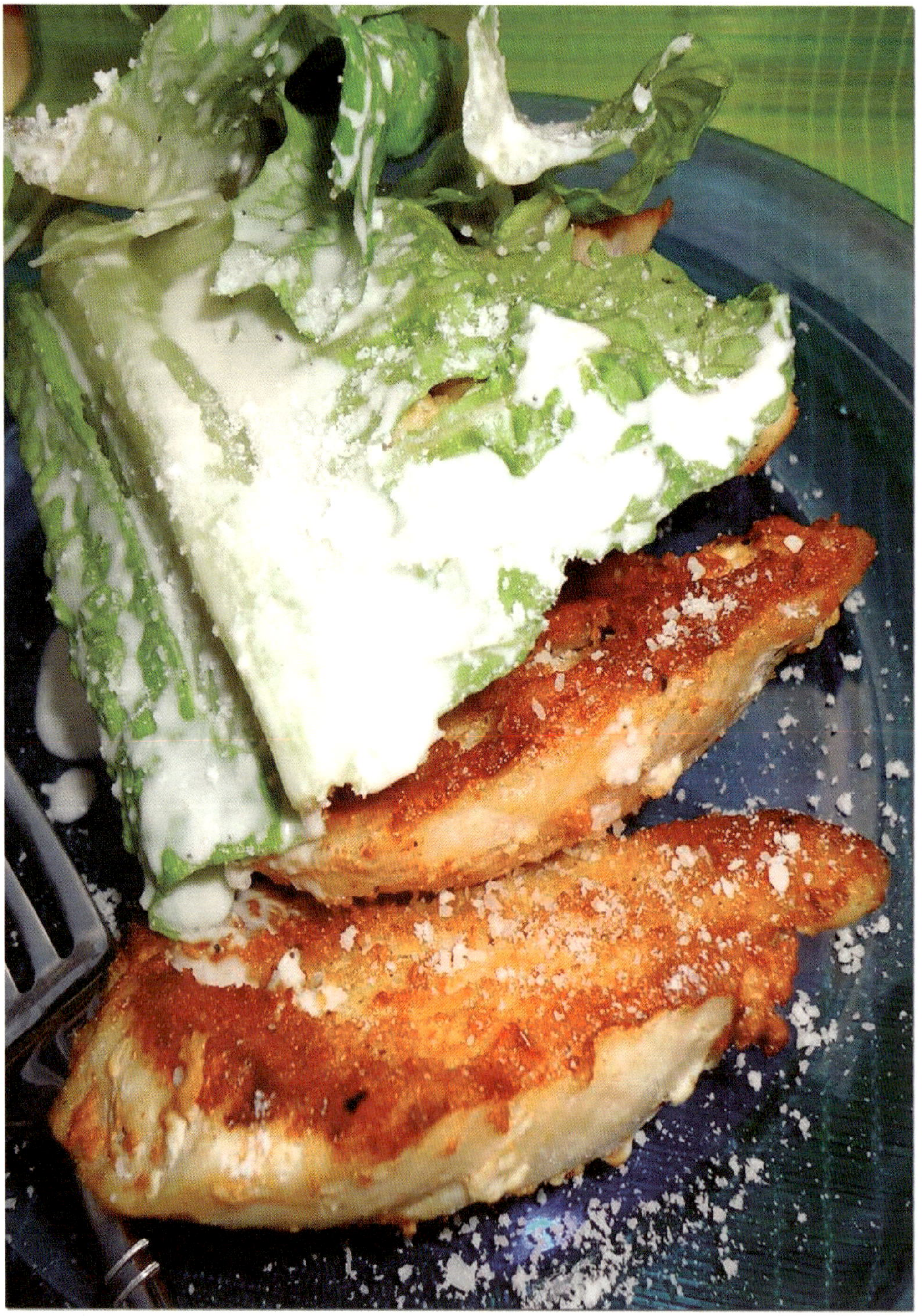

Greek Caesar Salad

Serves: 8
Prep Time: 20 min.
Cooking Time: 20 min.

1. Combine the first 9 ingredients and 1/4 tsp. pepper in a large bowl.
2. Add the lettuce, toss to coat.
3. Place the chicken between 2 sheets of plastic wrap and pound to 1/4" thickness.
4. Sprinkle with pepper.
5. Heat a grill pan over medium-high heat and coat with cooking spray.
6. Add the chicken and cook for 10 minutes on each side.
7. Remove from the pan and place 1/2 a chicken breast on each plate.
8. Top with salad and sprinkle with parmesan to garnish.

3 tbsp. plain reduced-fat greek yogurt
2 tbsp. grated parmesan cheese
4 tsp. lemon juice
1 tbsp. water
2 tsp. extra virgin olive oil
1 tsp. worcestershire sauce
1 tsp. Dijon mustard
1/2 tsp. anchovy paste
1 small garlic clove, minced
1/2 tsp. black pepper
4 c. romaine lettuce, large chop
4 boneless skinless chicken breasts
cooking spray

Percent Daily Values (DV) are based on a 2000 calorie diet

Calories	97.7	Protein	13.0g
Total Fats	3.0g	Potassium	220.6g
Sodium	110.8mg	Phosphorus	10.0%

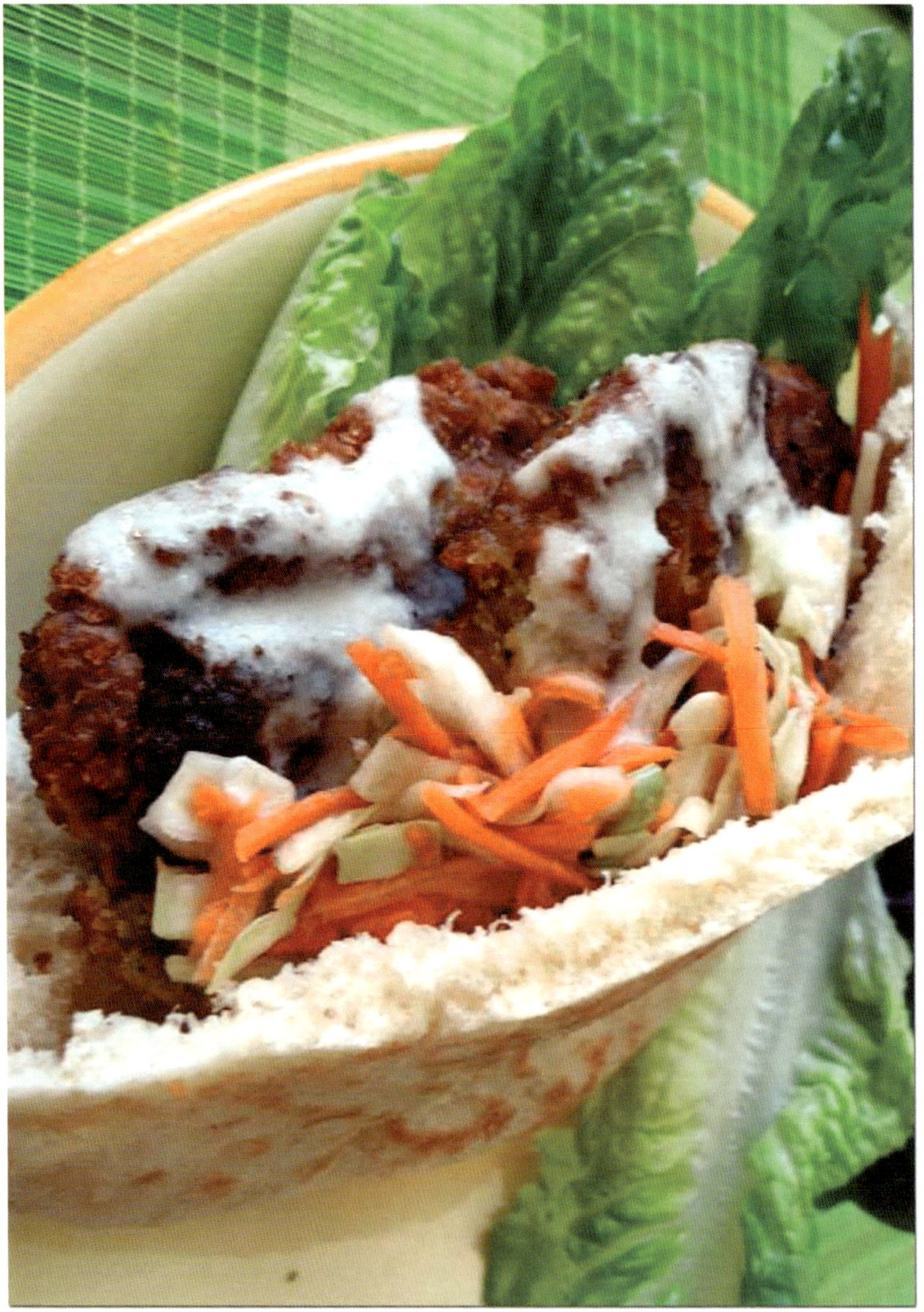

Chicken Pita Burgers

Serves: 8
Prep Time: 20 min.
Cooking Time: 10 min.

1. Combine the first 6 ingredients in a large bowl.
2. Add 1 tsp. of the lemon zest and stir well.
3. Divide mixture into 8 equal portions and form into patties.
4. Heat the oil in a large non-stick skillet over medium-high heat.
5. Add the patties to the skillet and cook for 2 minutes on each side.
6. Cover and reduce the heat to medium, cook for 5 minutes more.
7. Meanwhile, combine zest, yogurt, and oregano in a small bowl.
8. Fill each pita half with 1 patty and 1 tbsp. of the yogurt mixture.
9. Stuff each pita with the carrots, cabbage and lettuce.
10. Serve and Enjoy!

¡Qué rico!!

1/2 c. green onions, chopped
1/4 c. Italian breadcrumbs
1 tbsp. Greek no-salt seasoning blend
1/2 tsp. black pepper
2 large egg whites, lightly beaten
1 lb. extra-lean ground chicken
2 tsp. lemon zest
1 tbsp. olive oil
1/2 c. plain low-fat yogurt
1 1/2 tsp. oregano
4 pitas, cut in half
baby romaine lettuce
1 c. cabbage, shredded
1 c. carrots, shredded

Percent Daily Values (DV) are based on a 2000 calorie diet

Calories	228.4	Protein	15.4g
Total Fats	8.2g	Potassium	205.1g
Sodium	305.6mg	Phosphorus	6.2%

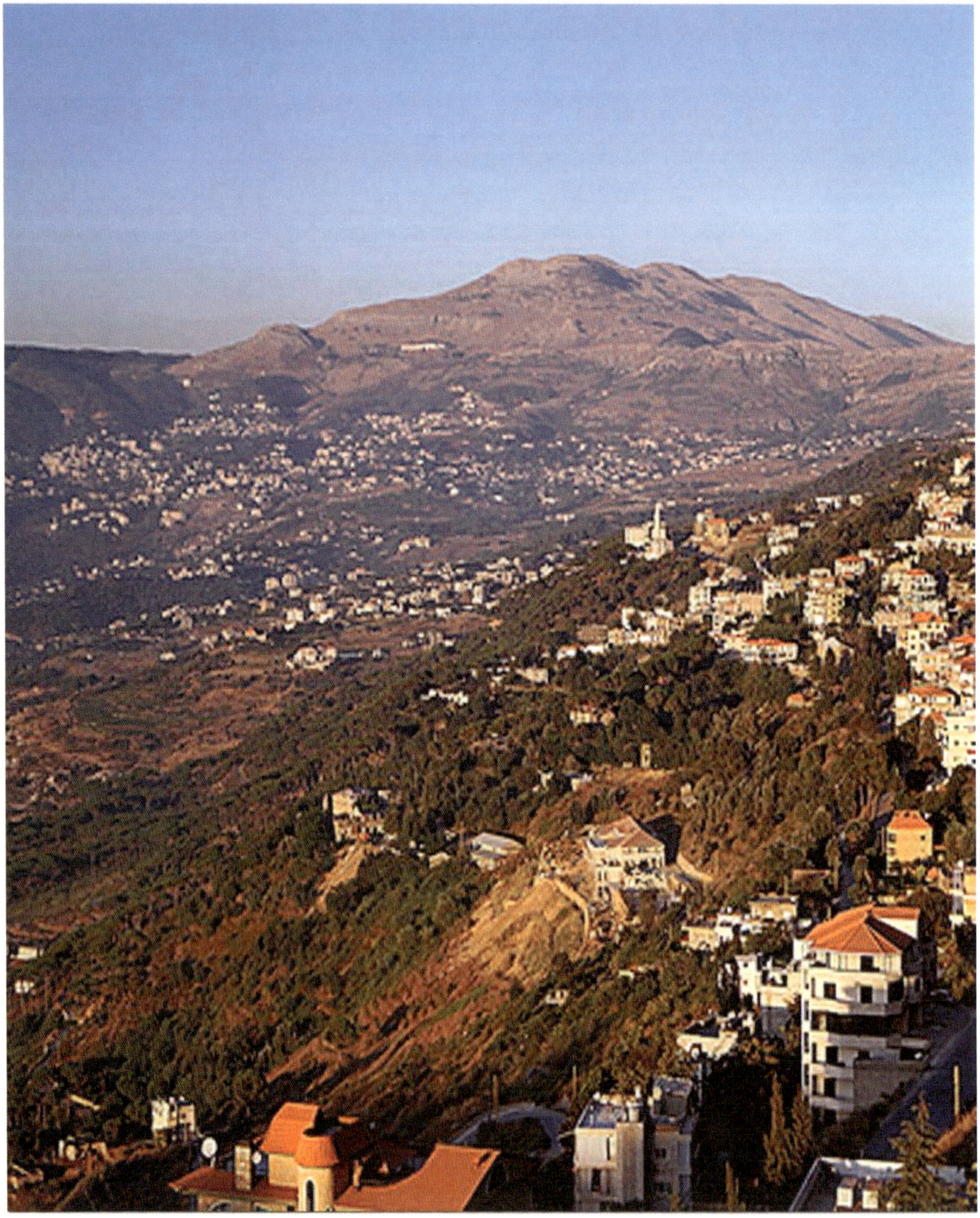

Lebanon

Lebanese food history is strongly influenced by cultures from foreign countries. Ottoman Turks brought olive oil, yogurt (laban), baklava and nuts. France brought flan, croissants and custards. Today the Lebanese enjoy a very Mediterranean diet.

105 | Lebanese Lamb Kabobs
107 | Stuffed Cabbage Rolls
109 | Lebanese Roasted Stuffed Onions
111 | Lebanese Eggplant Salad

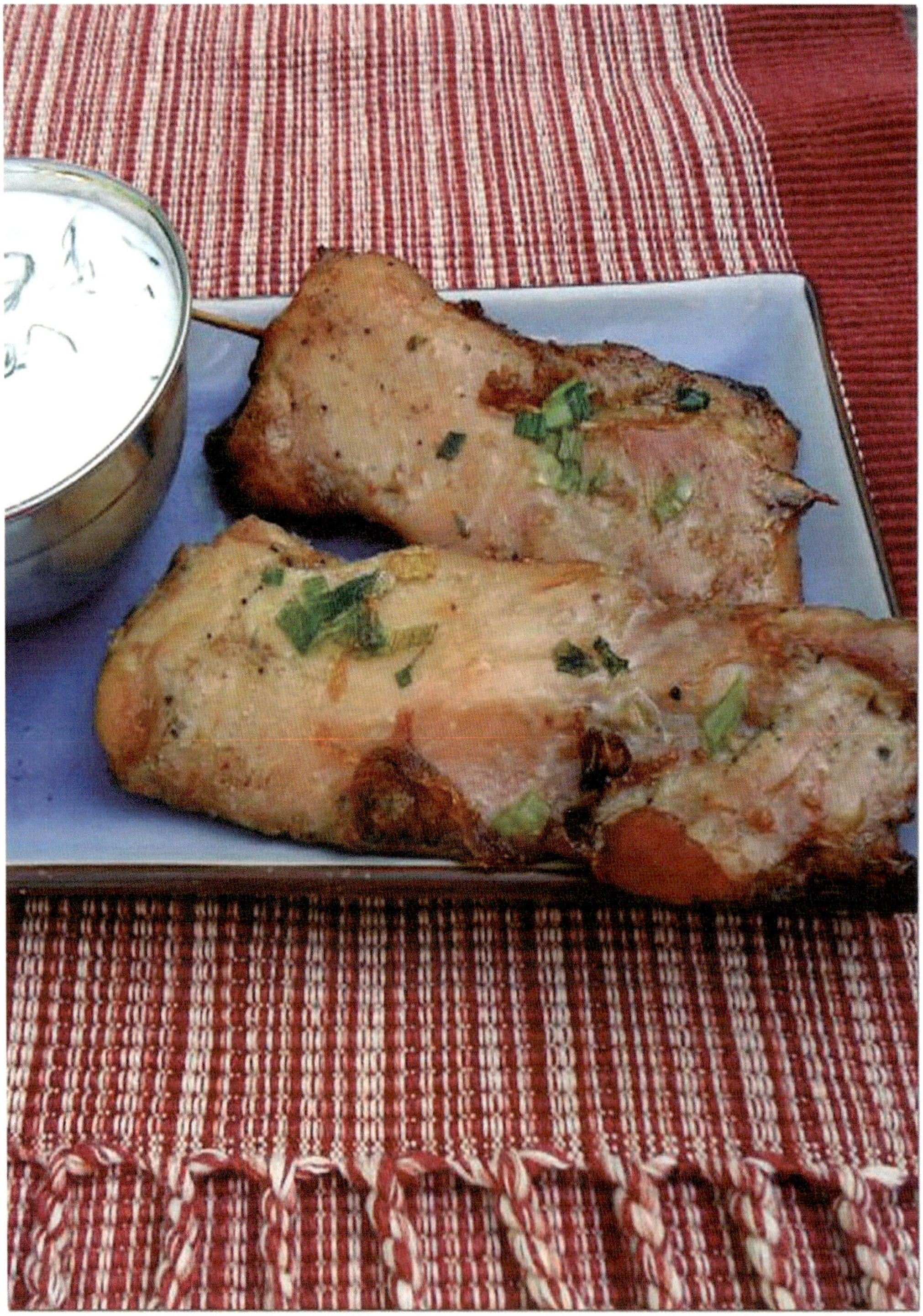

Lebanese Lamb Kabobs

Serves: 8
Prep Time: 15 min.
Cooking Time: 15 min.

1. In a large bowl, beat the eggs with a fork.
2. Stir in the onion, breadcrumbs, garlic, parsley, cilantro, oregano, mint, cumin, cinnamon and crushed red pepper.
3. Add the lamb and mix well.
4. Divide the mixture into 8 portions.
5. Shape each portion around a skewer forming a log about 6 inches long.
6. Place the skewers on a grill, and cook for 15 minutes or until done (160°F), turning once halfway through grilling.
7. In a small bowl, stir together the cucumber, yogurt and dill.
8. Serve alongside the kabobs.

Great for the BBQ!

2 eggs
1 small onion, finely chopped
1/2 c. soft breadcrumbs
4 cloves garlic, minced
2 tbsp. fresh parsley, chopped
1 tbsp. fresh cilantro, chopped
2 tsp. fresh oregano, chopped
2 tsp. fresh mint, chopped
1/2 tsp. ground cumin
1/2 tsp. ground cinnamon
1/4 tsp. crushed red pepper
1 1/2 lbs. ground lean lamb
soaked wooden skewers
1/2 cucumber, peeled, minced
3/4 c. plain yogurt
1/4 c. fresh dill, chopped

Percent Daily Values (DV) are based on a 2000 calorie diet

Calories	295.0	Protein	16.2g
Total Fats	13g	Potassium	241.3g
Sodium	128.1mg	Phosphorus	18.0%

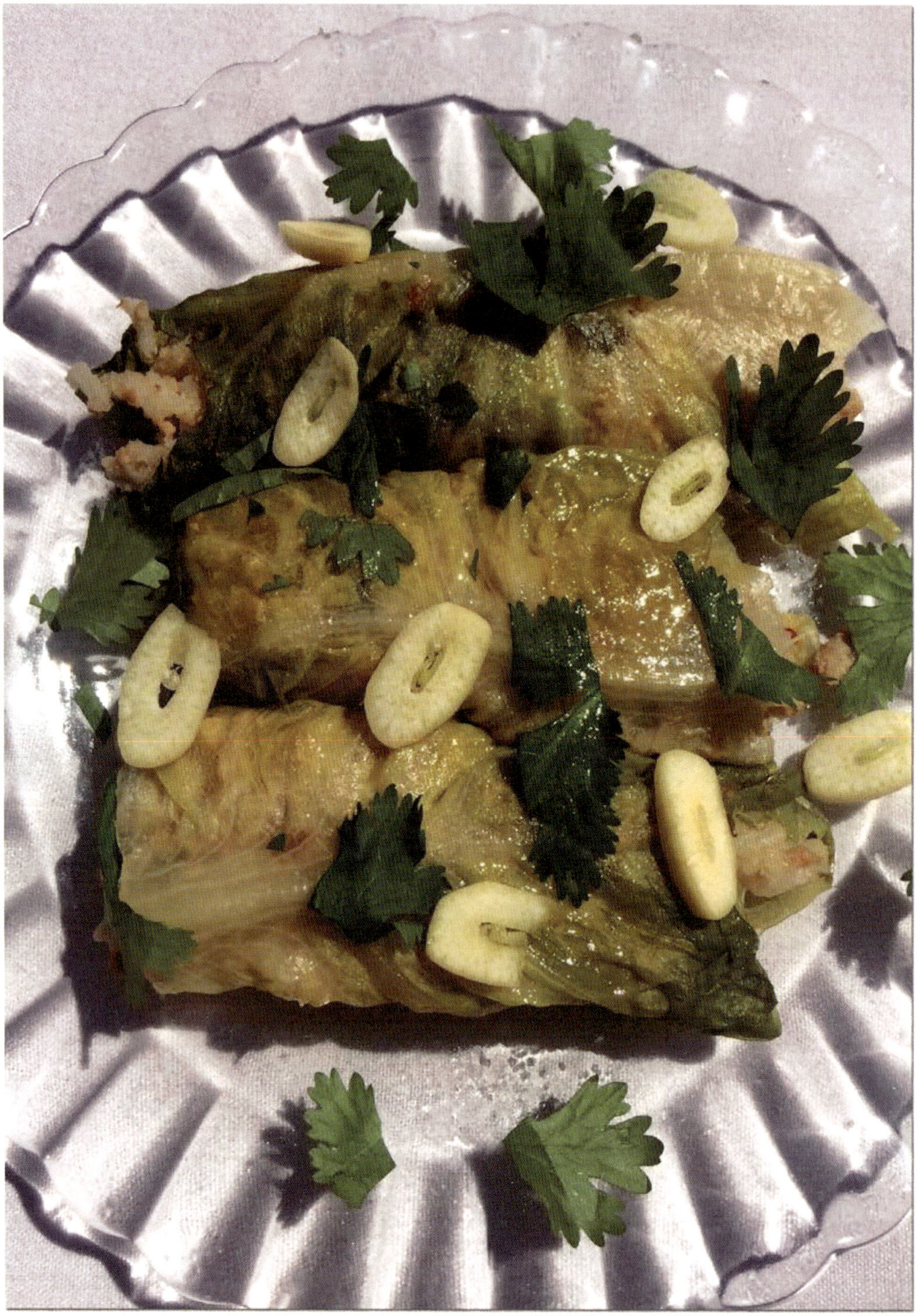

Stuffed Cabbage Rolls

Serves: 15 (2 rolls each)
Prep Time: 15 min.
Cooking Time: 20 min.

1. Peel and discard the outer leaves of the cabbage and separate the leaves.
2. In a steamer, steam the leaves for 3-4 minutes or until pliable.
3. Let cool and set aside.
4. In a large skillet, cook the ground beef over medium heat until no longer pink, drain.
5. Add lemon juice, 7 spice and rice. Mix well.
6. Lay each cabbage leaf separately on a cutting board.
7. Spread 1 to 2 tablespoons of meat stuffing along the edge of the leaf, then roll it slowly and tightly over the meat so a roll is formed.
8. Place cabbage rolls in a steamer and cook for 5 minutes.
9. Meanwhile, in a small skillet, add olive oil and garlic slices, sauté until tender.
10. Place cabbge rolls on serving plate and top with garlic.

1 head green cabbage
3/4 lb. lean ground beef
1 c. white rice, cooked
3 garlic cloves, sliced thinly
4 lemons, juiced
2 tsp. 7 spice
2 tbsp. olive oil

Great appetizer!

Percent Daily Values (DV) are based on a 2000 calorie diet

Calories	95.8	Protein	5.8g
Total Fats	4.4g	Potassium	288.1g
Sodium	28.5mg	Phosphorus	4.7%

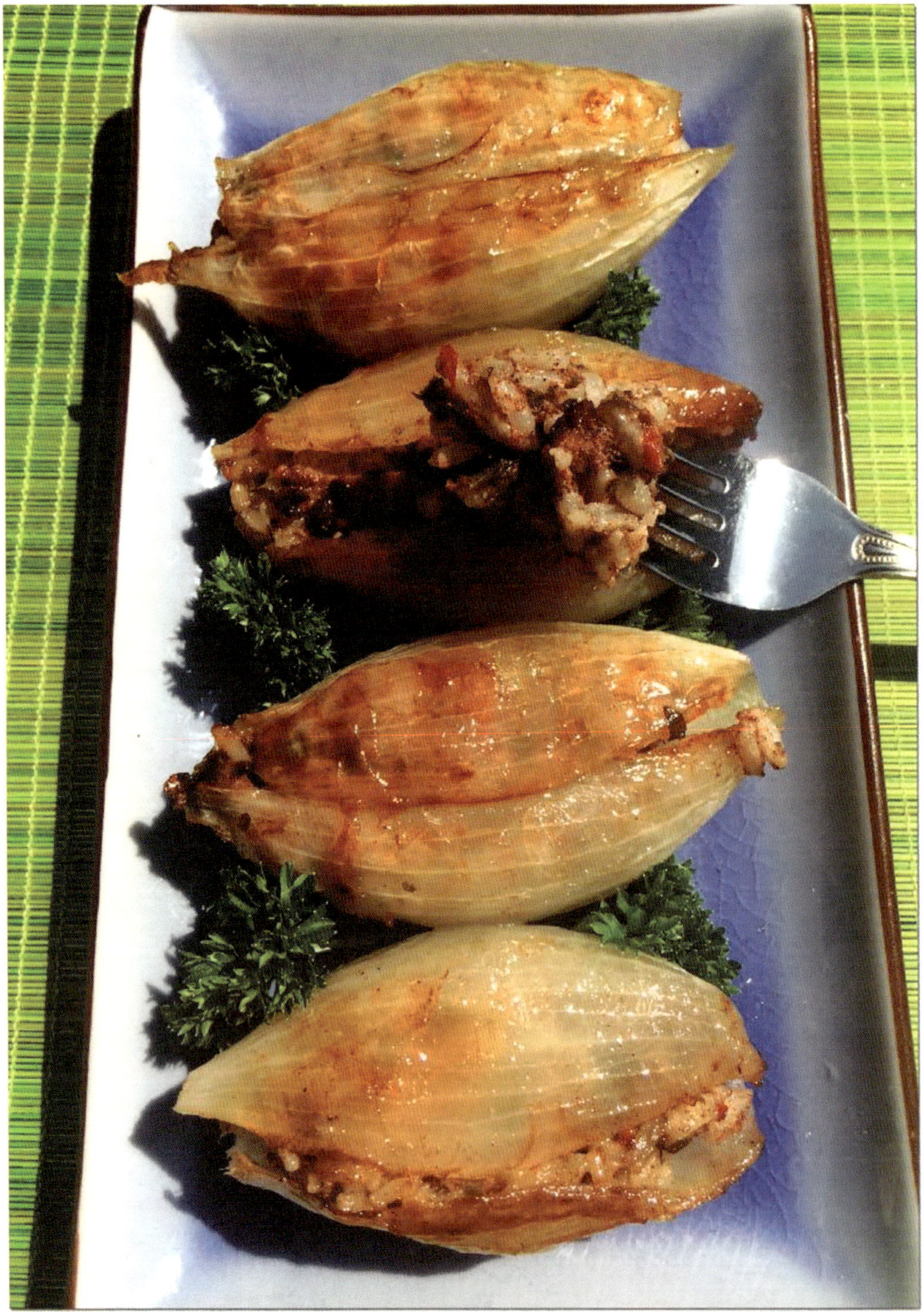

Lebanese Roasted Stuffed Onions

Serves: 10
Prep Time: 15 min.
Cooking Time: 45 min.

1. Cut off the top and bottom of each onion.
2. Make a cut down one side of each of the onions, cutting into the center from top to bottom.
3. In a large pot of boiling water, add the onions and cook for 10 minutes.
4. Meanwhile, in a large bowl add the rice, peppers, all the spices and herbs, and the ground meat. Mix well.
5. Remove the onions from the water and drain.
6. Let cool and separate the layers individually. Place one tablespoon of the filling in the onion and wrap around filling.
7. In a large skillet over medium-high heat, swirl in the olive oil.
8. Place the onions seam side down and cook for two minutes or until the bottoms have slightly browned.
9. Add the vinegar to the pan and sprinkle the tops of the onions with sugar.
10. Cover the pan and turn the heat to low.
11. Cook for 20 minutes, rotating the onions halfway through.

2 large onions

1 c. white rice, cooked

1 tbsp. roasted red peppers, pureed

2 tsp. cinnamon

1 tsp. all-spice

1 tsp. cumin

1 tsp. coriander

black pepper

3 tbsp. fresh cilantro, minced

3 tbsp. fresh parsley, minced

1 lb extra-lean ground pork

2 tbsp. cider vinegar

3 pinches sugar

1 tbsp. olive oil

Percent Daily Values (DV) are based on a 2000 calorie diet

Calories	141.4	Protein	8.9g
Total Fats	8.0g	Potassium	160.2g
Sodium	24.1mg	Phosphorus	8.8%

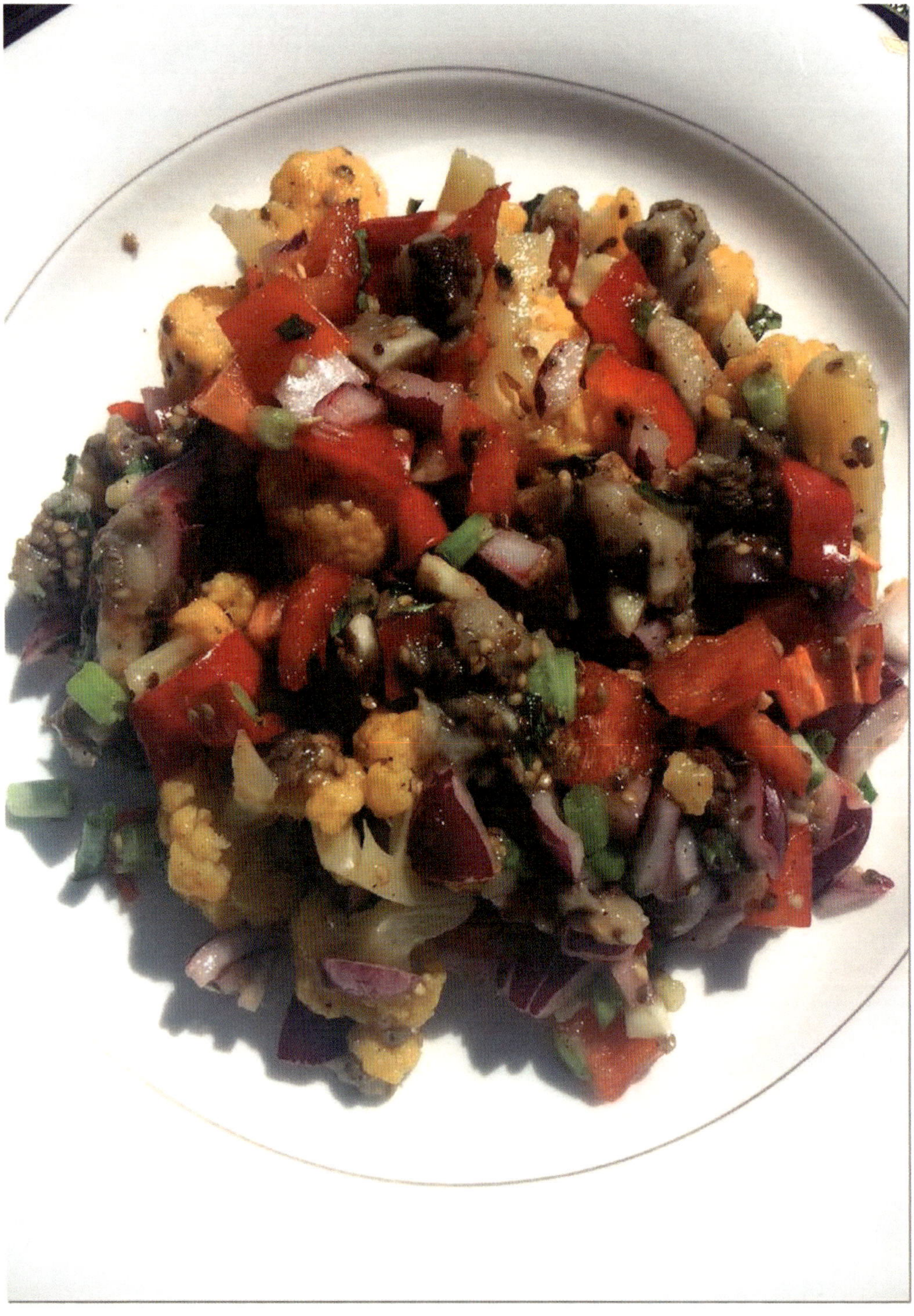

Lebanese Eggplant Salad

Serves: 4
Prep Time: 15 min.
Cooking Time: 30 min.

1. Preheat the oven to 350°F.
2. Put the whole eggplant and cauliflower on a lined baking sheet and bake for 30 minutes.
3. Remove from oven and let cool.
4. Dice the eggplant after removing the skin.
5. Put all the ingredients along with the roasted vegetables into a large bowl. Mix well and serve!

3 small eggplants
1 c. diced bell peppers
1/2 c. red onion, diced
1/2 c. cauliflower florets
1/2 c. scallions, chopped
1 clove garlic, minced
1/2 c. fresh parsley, chopped
juice of 1 lemon
1 tbsp. olive oil
pepper to taste

Eggplant lovers rejoice!

Percent Daily Values (DV) are based on a 2000 calorie diet

Calories	62.8	Protein	1.2g
Total Fats	3.6g	Potassium	121.0g
Sodium	70.8mg	Phosphorus	1.8%

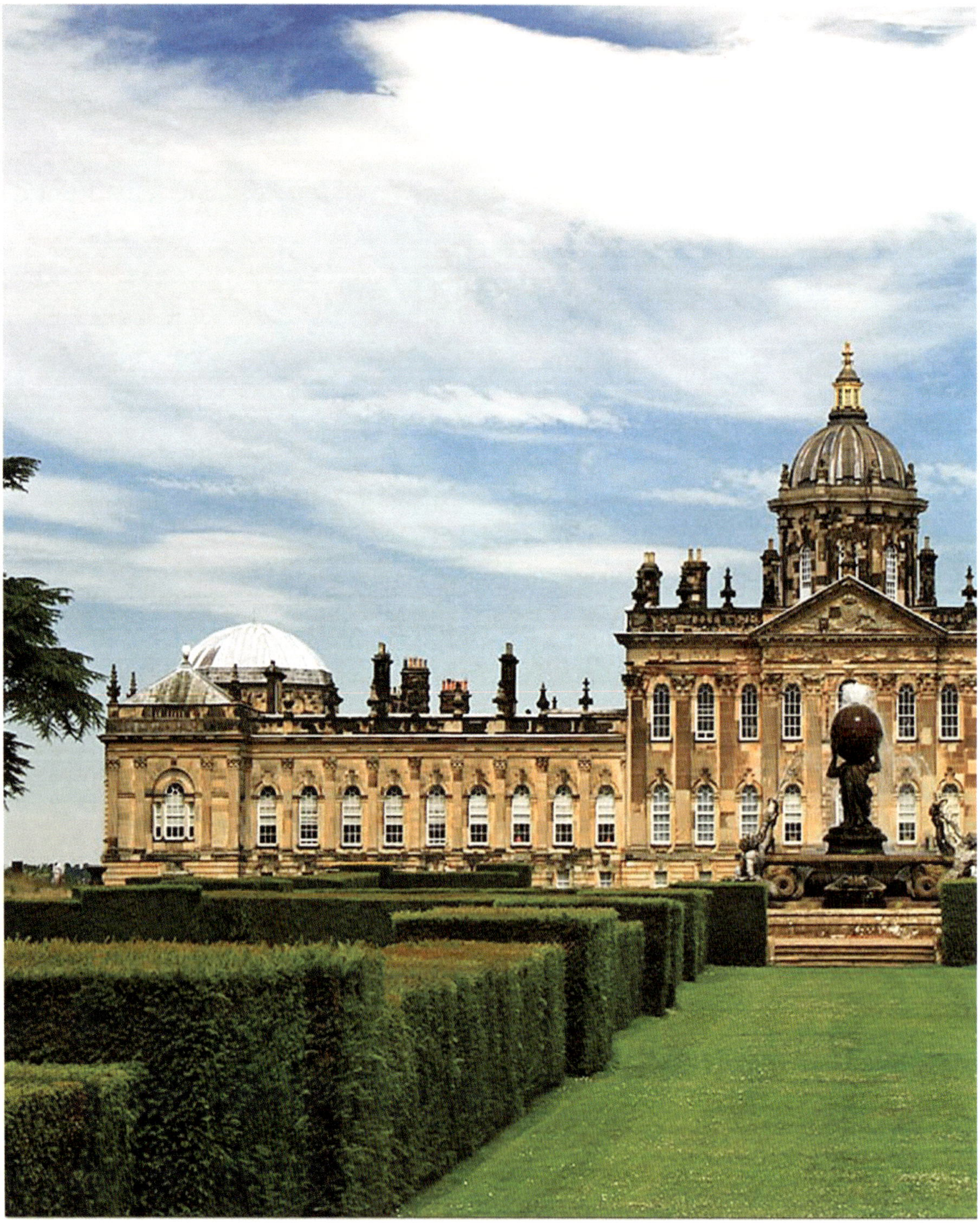

England

English cuisine is heavily influenced by foreign invaders. The Vikings, Romans and French brought a melting pot of different ingredients. English Fish & Chips, Roast Beef & Yorkshire Pudding and English Pasties are world renowned.

115 | Mustard Herbed Yorkies
117 | English Finger Sandwhiches
119 | English Meat Pies
121 | Old Fashioned Kedgeree
123 | Cauliflower Cottage Pie

113 | ENGLAND

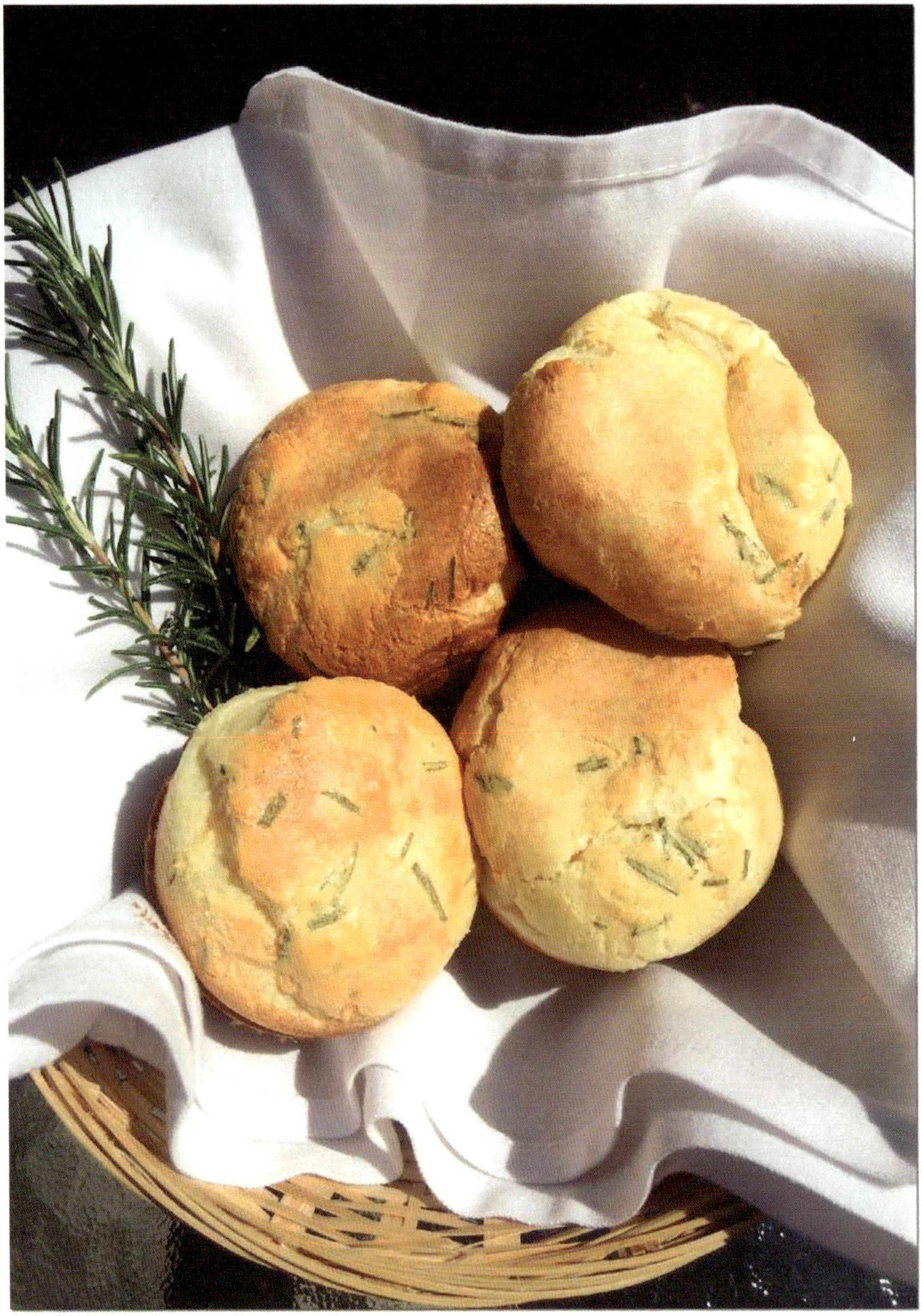

Mustard Herbed Yorkies

Serves: 12
Prep Time: 10 min.
Cooking Time: 20 min.

1. Preheat oven to 425°F.
2. In a blender, add the flour, eggs, milk, yellow mustard, rosemary and thyme.
3. Blend until nice and smooth.
4. Take a muffin pan and spray with cooking spray.
5. Place in the oven for 5 minutes to get nice and hot.
6. Remove the muffin pan from oven and fill greased muffin tins with batter (about 3/4 full).
7. Bake for 20 minutes.
8. Remove from oven and let cool on a wire rack. Serve warm.

Great for sloppin' up gravy!

1 1/2 c. all-purpose flour
5 eggs
1 1/2 c. non-fat milk
1/4 tsp. yellow mustard
1 tsp. chopped rosemary
1 tsp. chopped thyme
cooking spray

Percent Daily Values (DV) are based on a 2000 calorie diet

Calories	105.0	Protein	6.0g
Total Fats	2.7g	Potassium	99.3g
Sodium	51.2mg	Phosphorus	9.8%

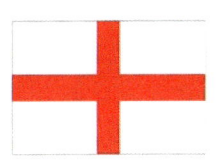

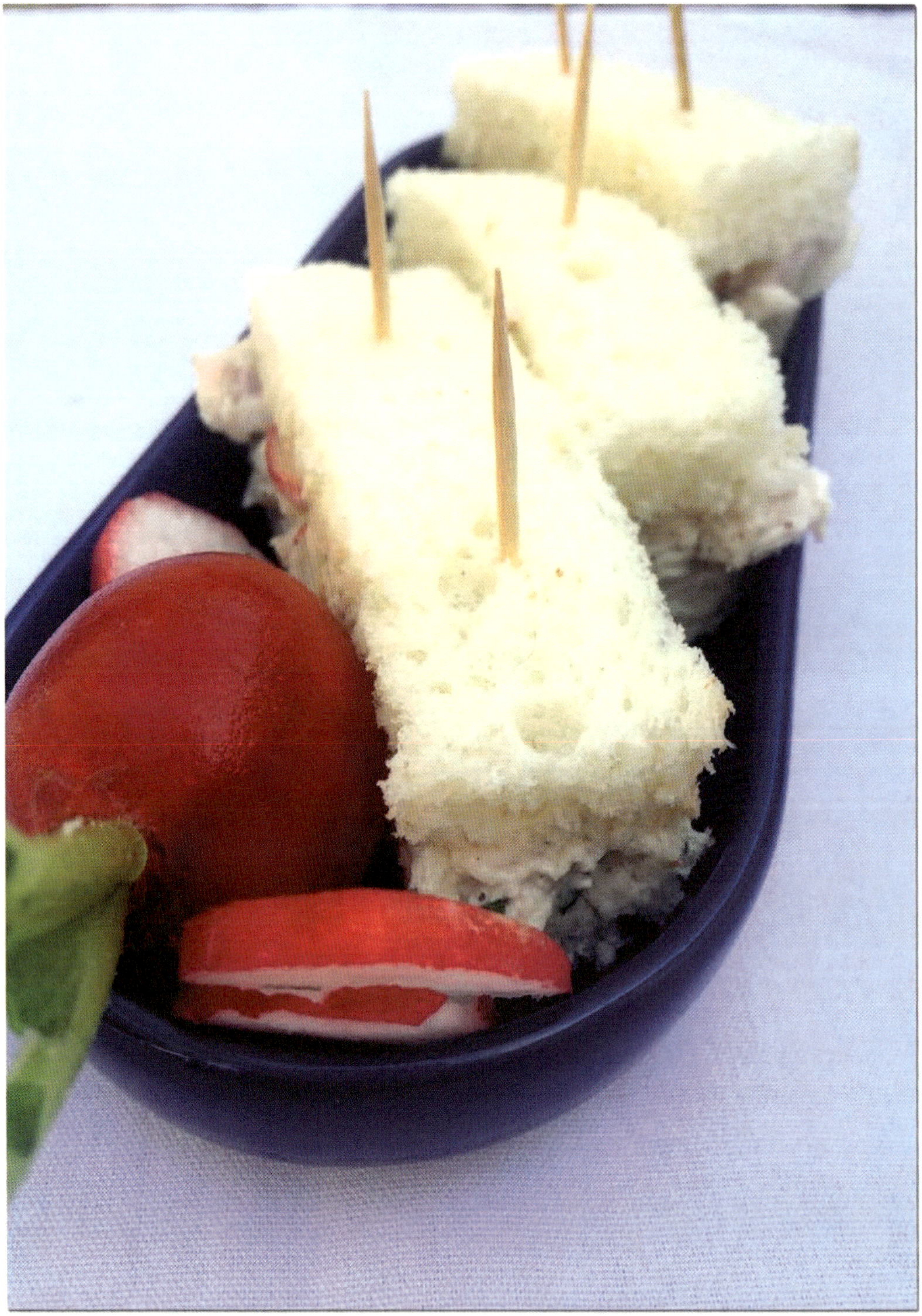

English Finger Sandwiches

Serves: 18
Prep Time: 15 min.
Cooking Time: -

1. Shred the chicken and place in a large bowl, along with the radish, mayonnaise, mint and pepper.
2. Stir until combined.
3. Place half the bread slices in a single layer on a clean and dry workspace.
4. Evenly spread the chicken mixture on each piece.
5. Top with remaining bread slices.
6. With a sharp knife, trim the crusts from each sandwich.
7. Cut each sandwich lengthways into thirds.
8. Secure with toothpicks and arrange on a platter to serve.

6 oz. skinless chicken breast, cooked
4 medium radishes, sliced thin
1/2 c. light mayonnaise
1/2 c. fresh mint, shredded
ground black pepper
12 slices white bread

Tea time!

Percent Daily Values (DV) are based on a 2000 calorie diet

Calories	47.5	Protein	2.8g
Total Fats	1.2g	Potassium	26.7g
Sodium	84.1mg	Phosphorus	2.6%

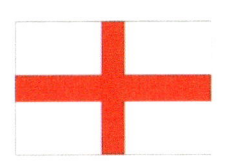

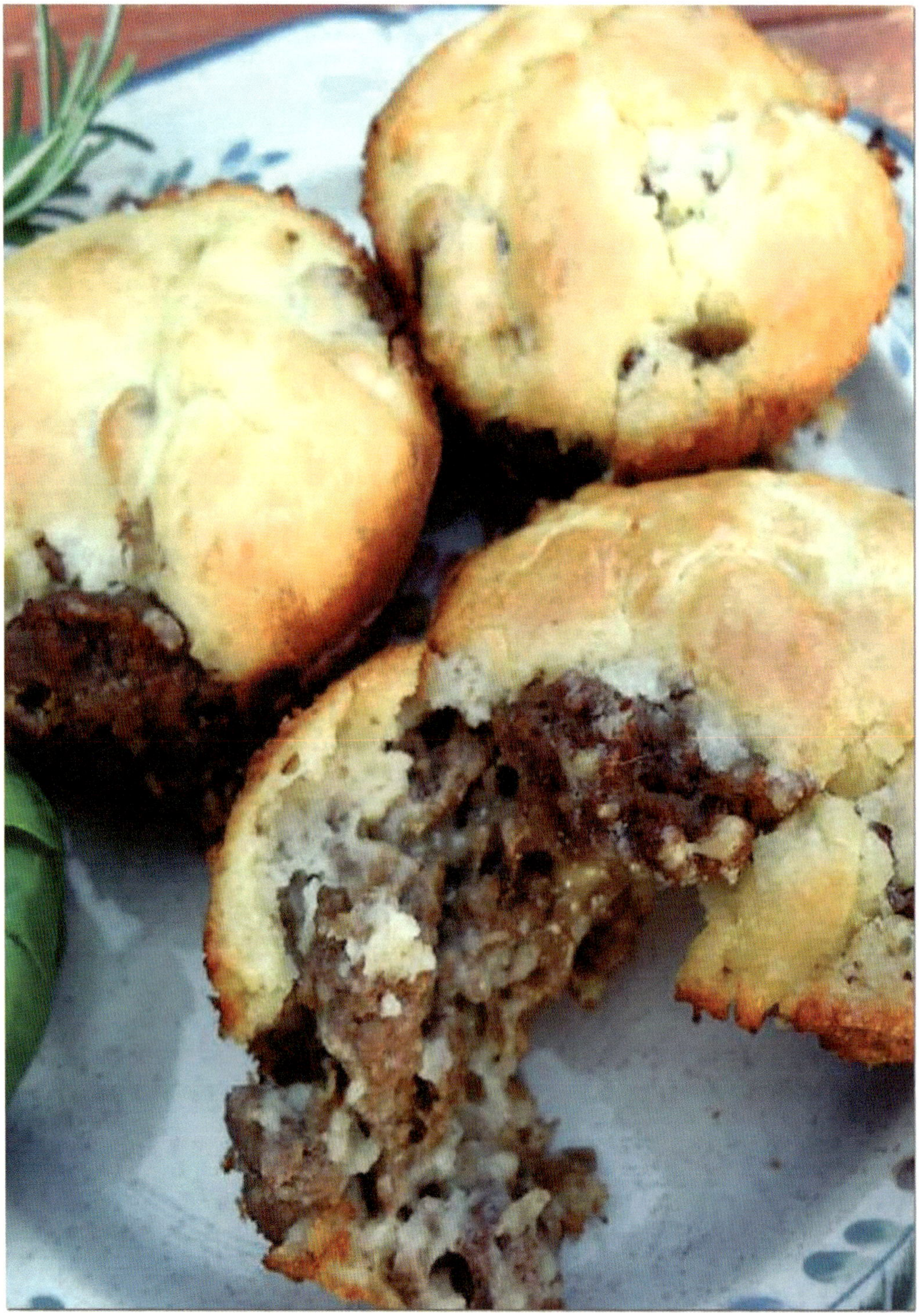

English Meat Pies

Serves: 12
Prep Time: 15 min.
Cooking Time: 20 min.

1. Preheat oven to 350°F.
2. In a skillet over medium heat, soften onions in the butter.
3. Add the beef and brown lightly and quickly so as not to overcook it.
4. Add mushrooms and sauté for 1 minute more.
5. Remove from heat, let cool.
6. Mix in the breadcrumbs, egg, and pepper and set aside.
7. Cut both pastry sheets into 12 equal squares, for a total of 24.
8. In a muffin pan, line each cup with a pastry square.
9. Divide the meat mixture into each lined cup.
10. Top with remaining pastry squares and press down slightly to seal.
11. Bake for 20 minutes or until browned on top.
12. Remove from oven and cool pies for 5 minutes.
13. With a knife, loosen sides of pies and place on wire rack to cool.

1 lb. lean ground beef

1 tbsp. unsalted butter

1/4 c. onions, chopped

1 tbsp. mushrooms, chopped

1/4 c. soft breadcrumbs

1 egg beaten

prepared pastry for a 2 crust pie

pepper to taste

Percent Daily Values (DV) are based on a 2000 calorie diet

Calories	290.0	Protein	16.0g
Total Fats	18.2g	Potassium	235.9g
Sodium	118.3mg	Phosphorus	13.8%

119 | ENGLAND

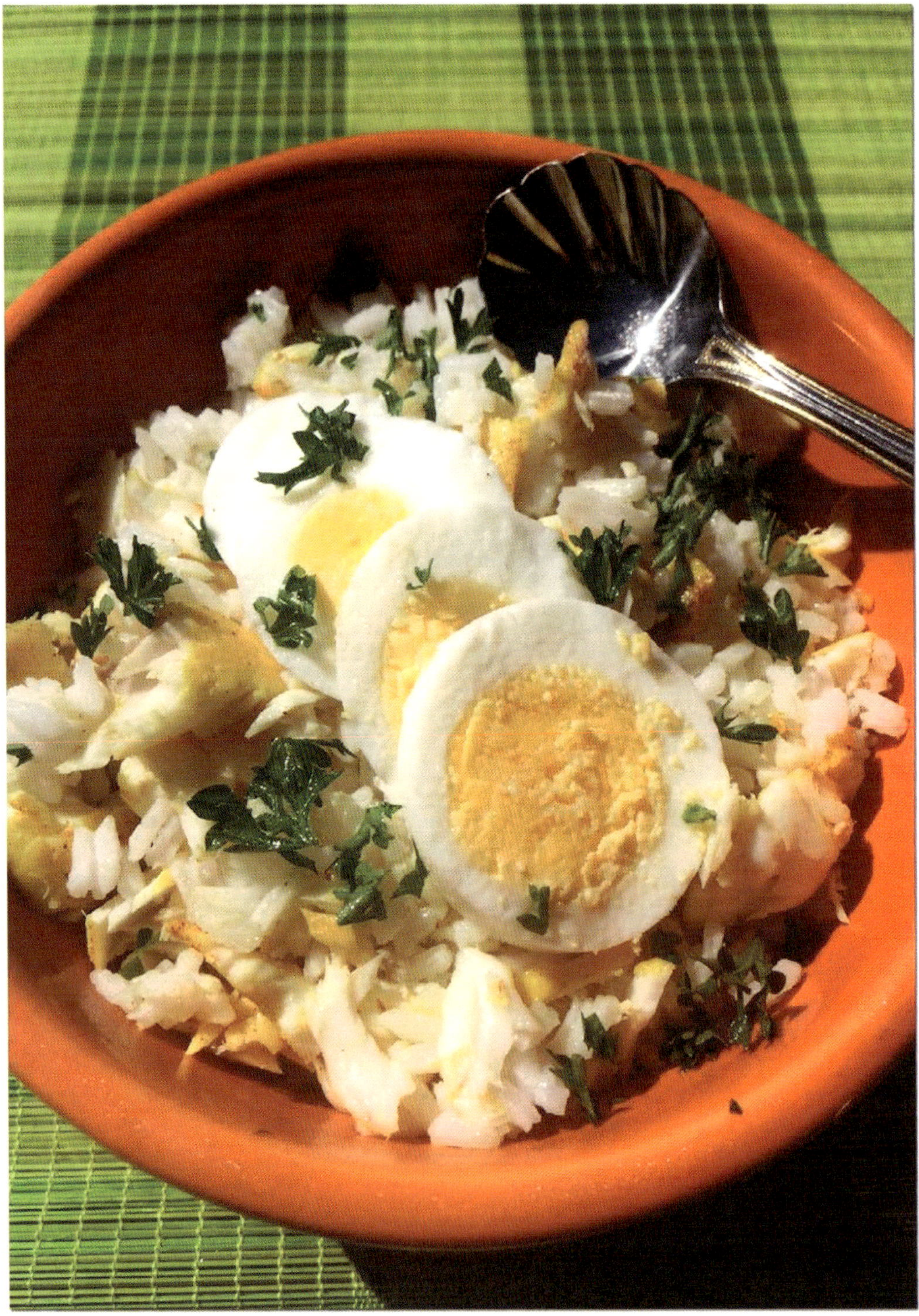

Old-Fashioned Kedgeree

Serves: 4
Prep Time: 15 min.
Cooking Time: 40 min.

1. Cook the rice in a saucepan of fast boiling water until tender, about 15 minutes.
2. Drain and rinse under cold water.
3. Spread out on a baking sheet to dry.
4. Meanwhile, poach the haddock in a large skillet of simmering water for 15 minutes or until tender.
5. Drain, skin and flake the haddock with a fork.
6. Chop one egg and slice the other into rings.
7. Melt the butter in a saucepan, add the rice, fish and chopped egg.
8. Season with pepper, and cook over medium heat for 3 minutes, stirring frequently.
9. Pile onto a warm serving dish and garnish with parsley and the sliced egg.

1 c. long-grain rice
1 lb. smoked haddock filets
2 eggs, hard-boiled, shelled
1 tbsp. unsalted butter
chopped fresh parsley

Hearwarming!

Percent Daily Values (DV) are based on a 2000 calorie diet

Calories	190.2	Protein	19.3g
Total Fats	4.6g	Potassium	56.3g
Sodium	130.6mg	Phosphorus	7.2%

ENGLAND

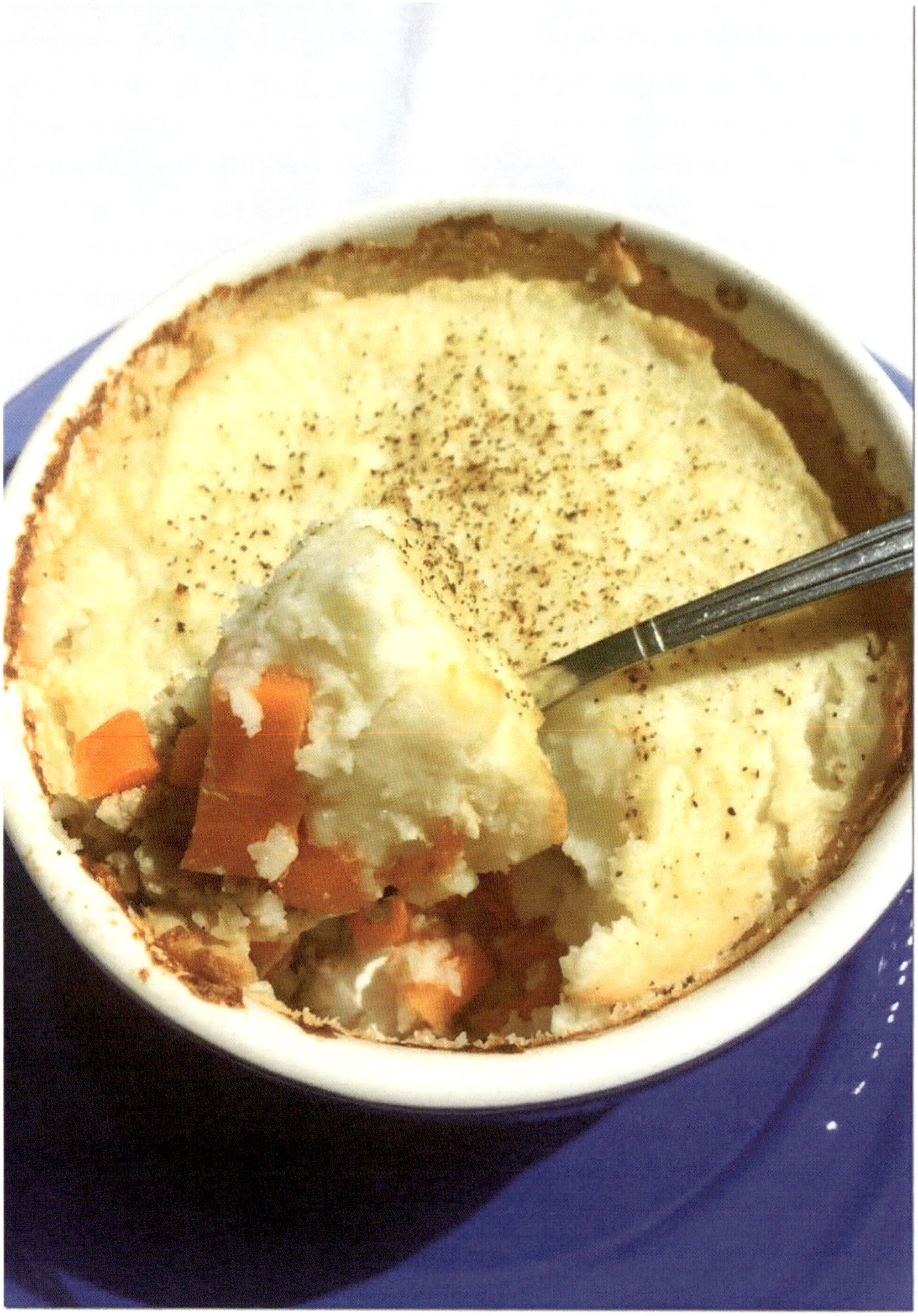

Cauliflower Cottage Pie

Serves: 8
Prep Time: 20 min.
Cooking Time: 30 min.

1. Preheat the oven to 350°F.
2. In a large skillet over medium heat, sauté the onions for 2 minutes.
3. Add the ground beef and sauté 5 more minutes or until browned and drain.
4. Add the carrots, thyme, water, kitchen bouquet and worcestershire sauce.
5. Bring to a boil and reduce to a simmer.
6. Cook until all the water has been absorbed.
7. Remove from heat and set aside.
8. Fill a large saucepan with water and bring to a boil.
9. Cook the cauliflower for 5-6 minutes or until fork tender. Drain.
10. In a large bowl, add the cauliflower, white pepper, nutmeg and almond milk. Mash together until smooth.
11. In a large casserole dish or small ramekins, layer the meat and veggie mixture and top with the cauliflower mash.
12. Bake for 30 minutes or until browned on top.

1 lb. lean ground beef

2 small yellow onions, peeled, chopped

1 tsp. dried thyme

1 c. water

1 tbsp. kitchen bouquet browning and seasoning sauce

1 tbsp. worcestershire sauce

2 lbs. cauliflower

1/8 tsp. white pepper

1/8 tsp. nutmeg

1/4 c. almond milk

black pepper to taste

Percent Daily Values (DV) are based on a 2000 calorie diet

Calories	101.2	Protein	6.0g
Total Fats	6.3g	Potassium	175.7g
Sodium	49.7mg	Phosphorus	5.7%

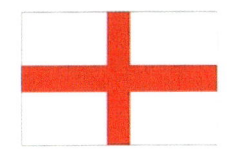

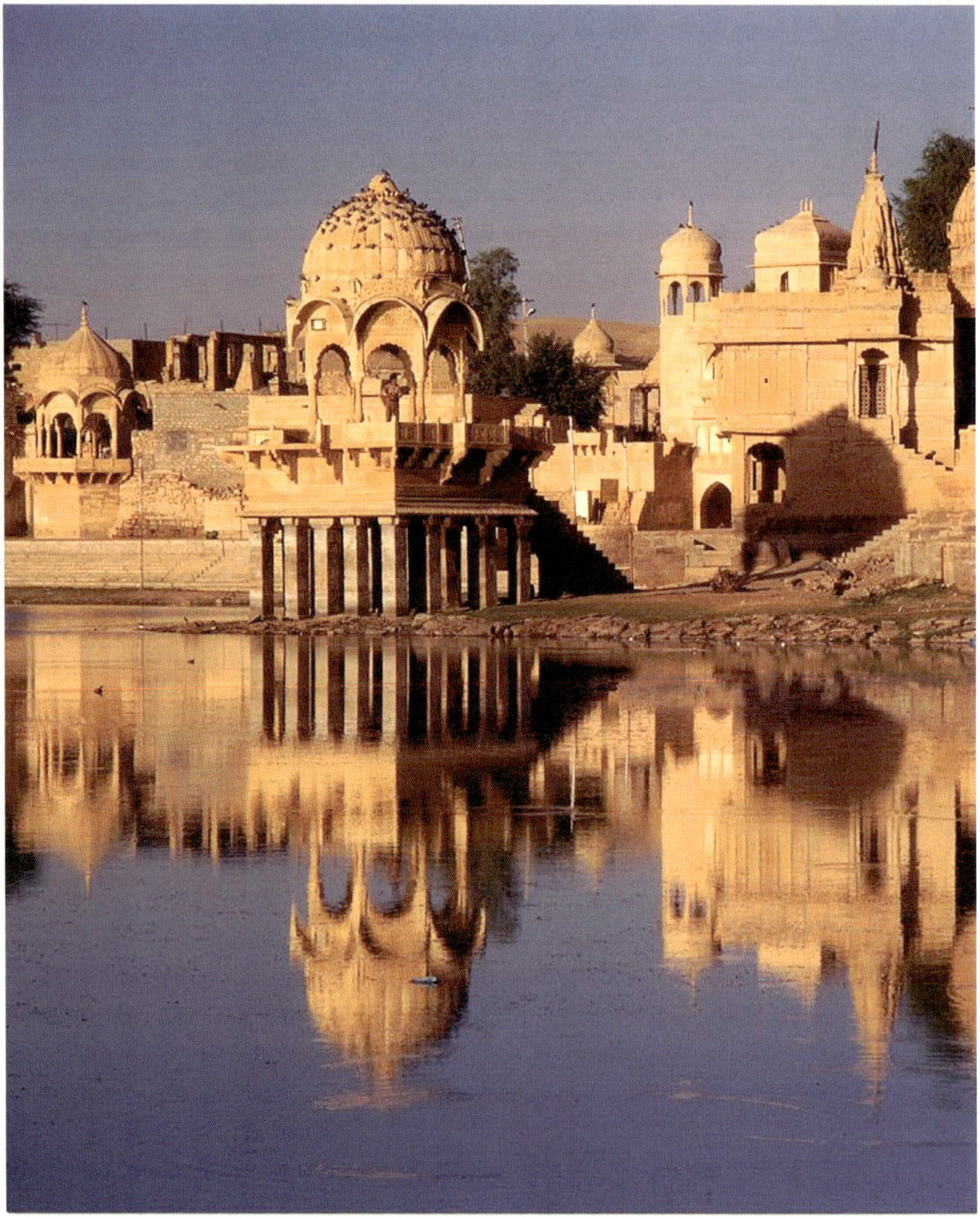

India

Regions and lifestyles make up a large portion of the cultural makeup of the food of India. Indian cuisine is very commonly known as a sweet cuisine due to the fact that almost half its dishes are either sweets or desserts. In addition, the food of India is also heavily based on potatoes combined with many different spices.

127 | Chilled Carrot and Cauliflower Soup
129 | Indian Spiced Cauliflower
131 | Indian Vegetable Curry
133 | Chettinad Chicken

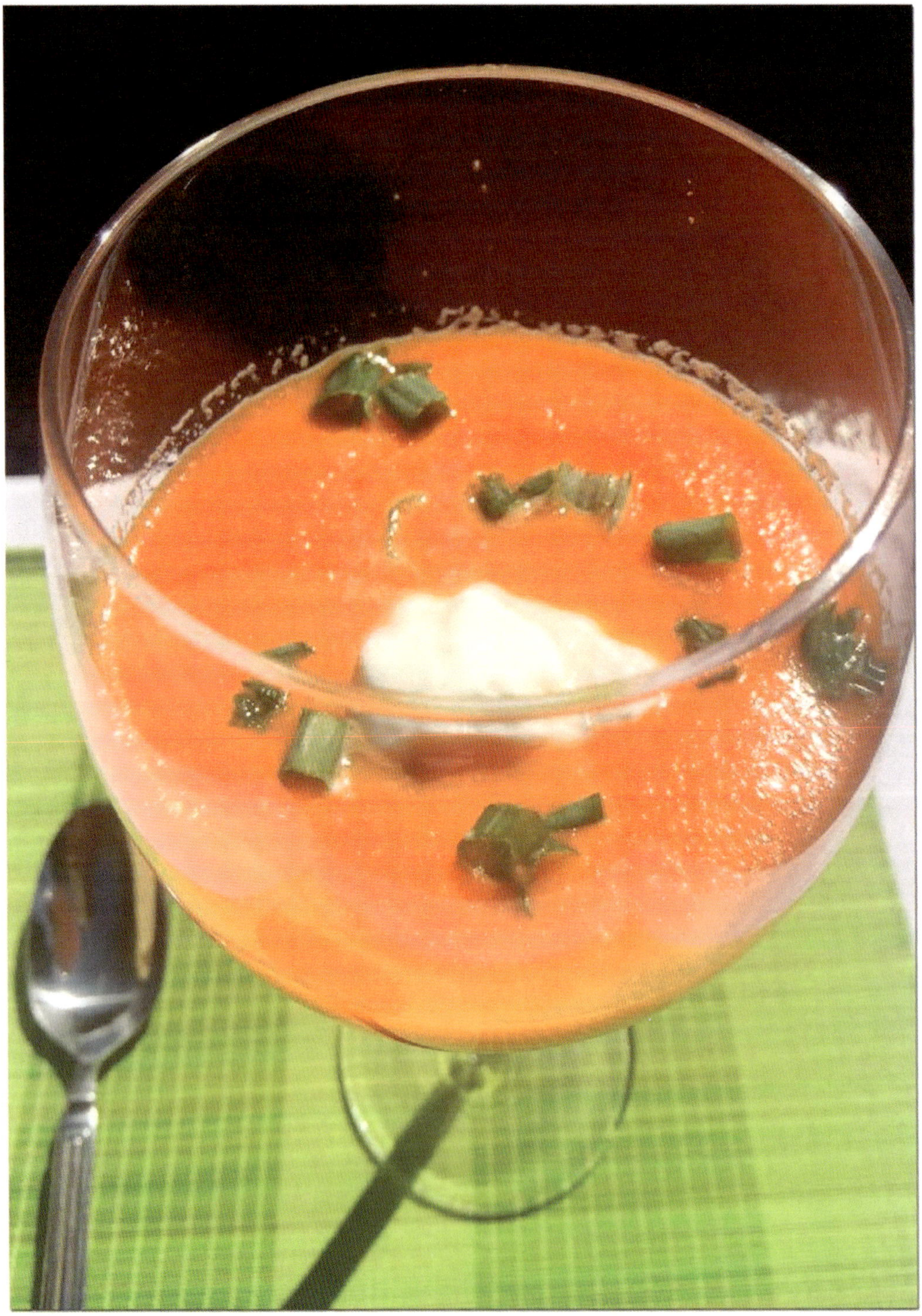

Chilled Carrot and Cauliflower Soup

Serves: 4
Prep Time: 10 min.
Cooking Time: 45 min.

1. Heat the oil in a large pot over medium heat.
2. Add the onions and cook for 5 minutes.
3. Add the carrots, cauliflower, red pepper flakes, lemon zest, cumin, turmeric, stock and bring to a boil.
4. Cover and simmer for 30 minutes.
5. Let the soup cool, and blend until smooth.
6. Pour the soup into a large bowl, and whisk in yogurt.
7. Season with pepper.
8. Chill the soup in the refrigerator for 2 hours.
9. Serve the soup in bowls with a dollop of yogurt and some chopped green onion.

Pass the Naan!

1/2 head cauliflower, chopped
2 c. carrots, peeled, sliced
1 tbsp. olive oil
1 yellow onion, chopped
2 c. non-fat low-sodium chicken stock
1/2 tsp. red pepper flakes
2 tsp. lemon zest
1 tsp. ground cumin
1 tsp. turmeric
1 green onion, finely chopped
3/4 c. low-fat plain yogurt
ground black pepper

Percent Daily Values (DV) are based on a 2000 calorie diet

Calories	71.5	Protein	4.4g
Total Fats	1.6g	Potassium	280.8g
Sodium	135.0mg	Phosphorus	7.2%

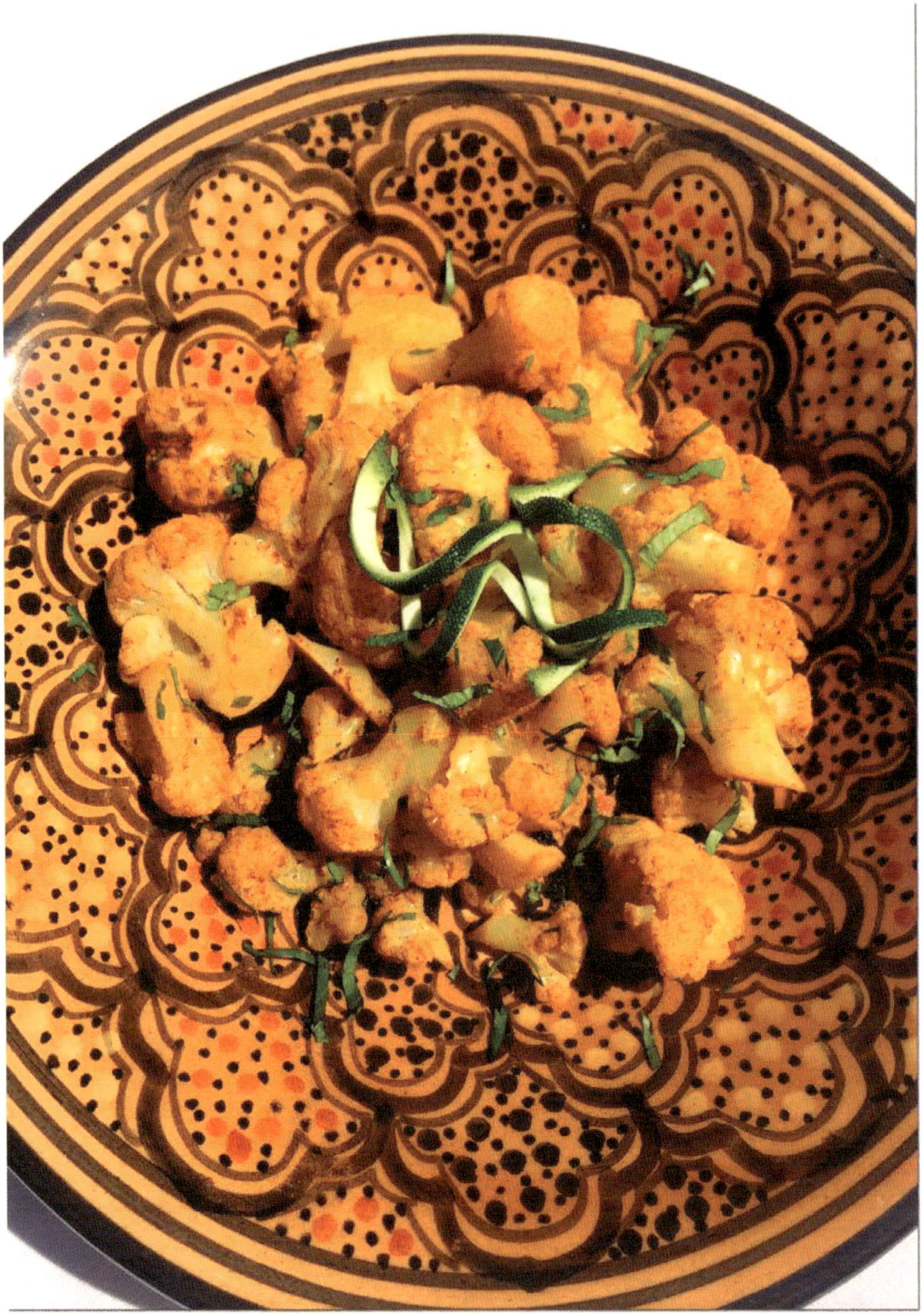

Indian Spiced Cauliflower

Serves: 8
Prep Time: 10 min.
Cooking Time: 10-15 min.

1. Preheat oven to 450°F.
2. In a large bowl, combine the cauliflower, olive oil, coriander, cumin, curry powder, turmeric and black pepper.
3. Toss well to combine.
4. On a lined baking sheet, spread the spiced cauliflower evenly.
5. Bake for 10-15 minutes or until the cauliflower or until edges are browned.
6. Remove from oven and top with the ginger, lime zest and fresh cilantro.

So healthy!

1 large head cauliflower, cut into florets
1 tbsp. olive oil
1 tsp. ground coriander
1 tsp. ground cumin
1 tsp. curry powder
1 tsp. turmeric powder
black pepper to taste
1 tsp. fresh ginger, grated
1 tsp. lime zest
fresh cilantro for garnish

Percent Daily Values (DV) are based on a 2000 calorie diet

Calories	25.7	Protein	0.7g
Total Fats	2.0g	Potassium	63.4g
Sodium	5.4mg	Phosphorus	1.4%

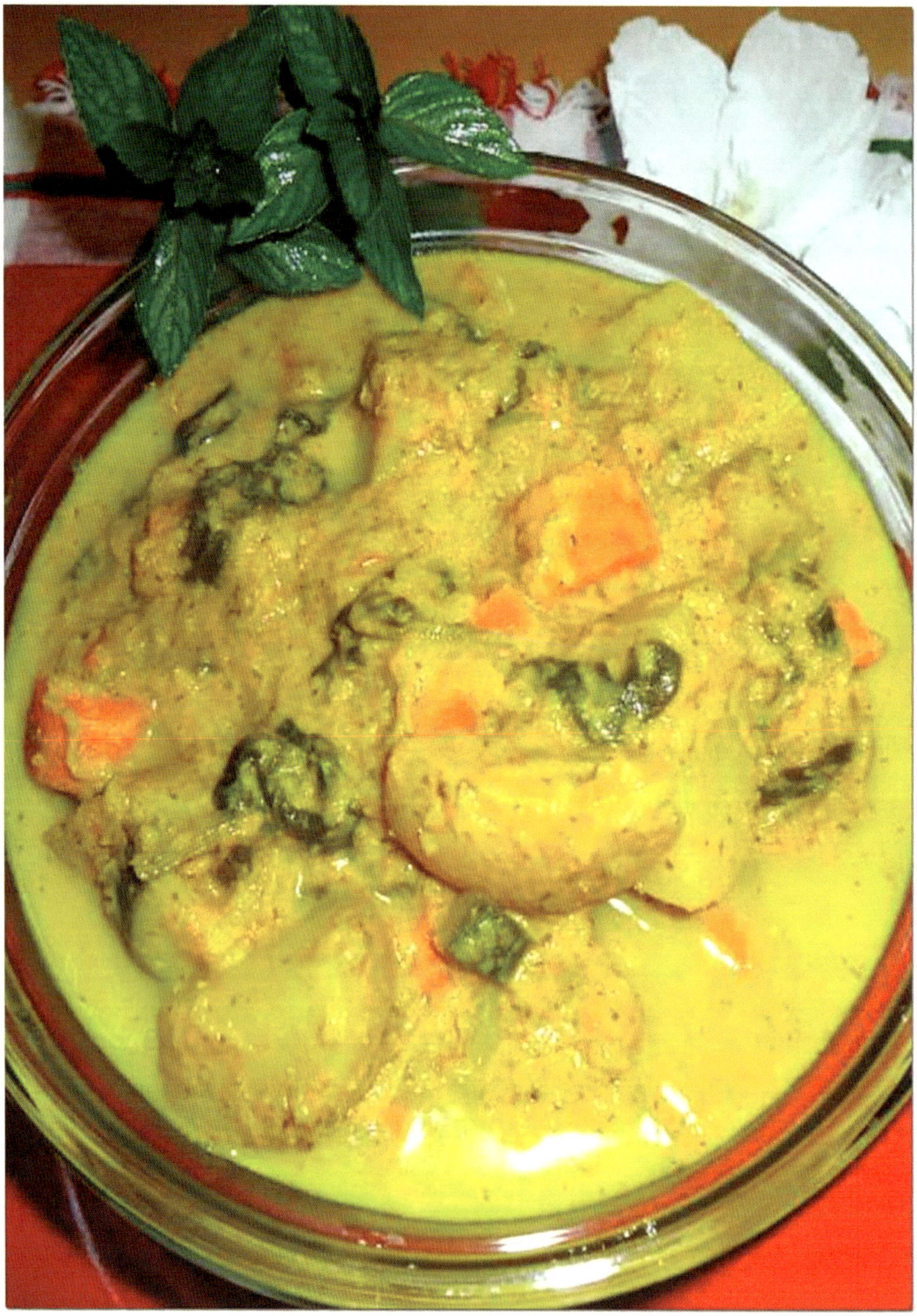

Indian Vegetable Curry

Serves: 4
Prep Time: 30 min.
Cooking Time: 30 min.

1. In a large saucepan, heat the oil over medium heat.
2. Add the peppercorns, cinnamon, cloves and onions, cook for 4 minutes.
3. Add the curry leaves, chilies, and ginger. Cook for 1 more minute.
4. Add the cauliflower, carrots, potatoes, and enough water to cover all the ingredients.
5. Bring the mixture to a boil and cook for 5 more minutes or until all the veggies are al denté.
6. Add the green beans, coconut milk, garam masala and turmeric and simmer gently for 10 minutes.
7. Garnish with cilantro and fresh mint!

Delicious with rice noodles!

2 c. leached potatoes, peeled, chopped
1 1/2 tbsp. coconut oil
20 black peppercorns
1 cinnamon stick
2 cloves
1 small onion, chopped
10 curry leaves
5 whole green chilies
1/2" piece fresh ginger, peeled, chopped
1 c. cauliflower, chopped
2 c. carrots, sliced
1/2 c. fresh green beans, chopped
1 c. coconut milk
1 tsp. garam masala
1 tsp. turmeric
handful fresh mint, chopped

Percent Daily Values (DV) are based on a 2000 calorie diet

Calories	189.4	Protein	4.0g
Total Fats	2.2g	Potassium	175.5g
Sodium	254.1mg	Phosphorus	5.8%

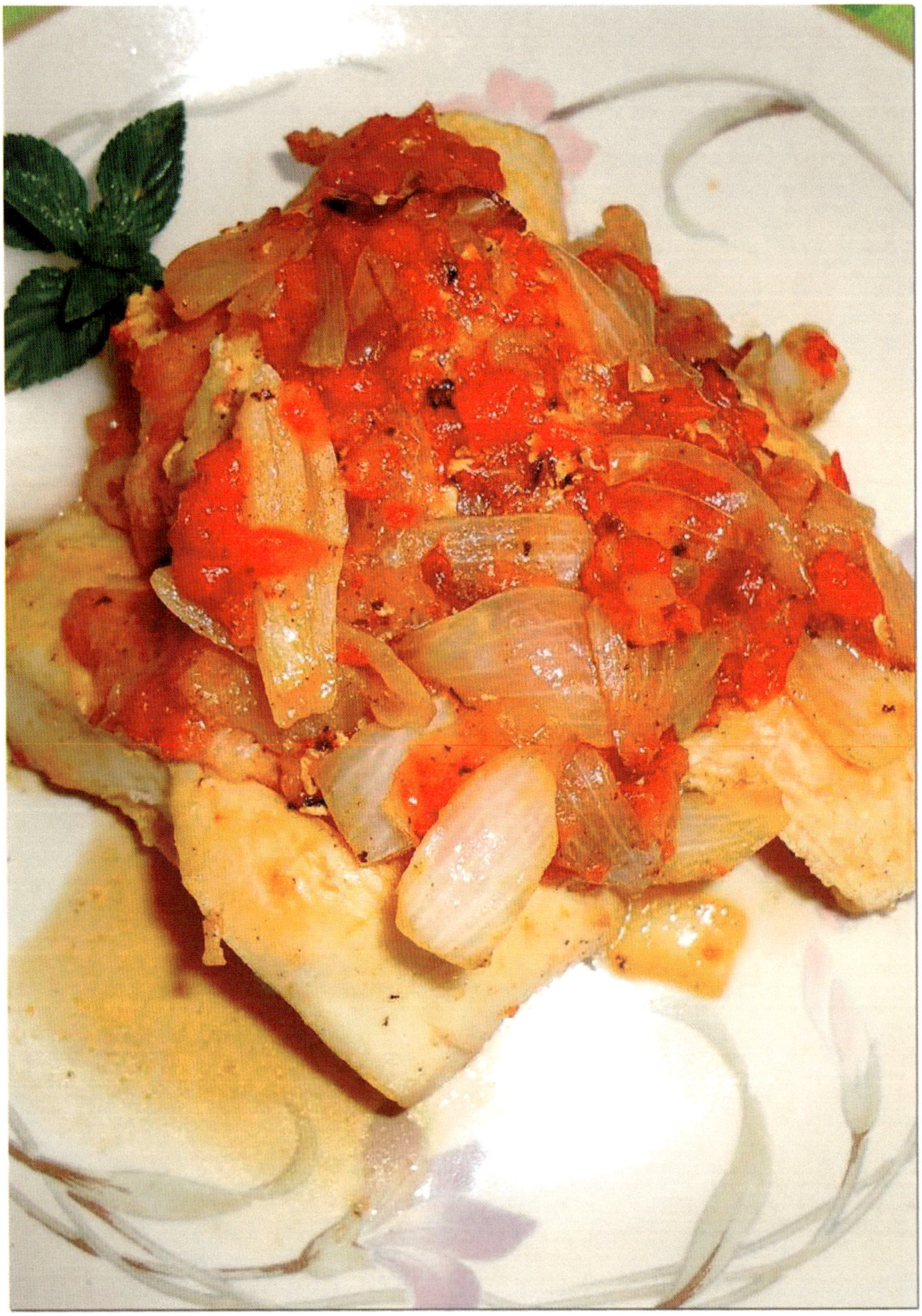

Chettinad Chicken

Serves: 8
Prep Time: 20 min.
Cooking Time: 55 min.

1. In a skillet, heat the oil over medium heat.
2. Add the cinnamon, bay leaf, fennel and cumin seeds.
3. Fry until brown.
4. Add the onion, pepper, garlic, ginger and turmeric.
5. Stir-fry until onions are tender.
6. Add the chicken to the pan and sear on all sides.
7. Reduce heat and add the curry powder, cayenne, black pepper and cumin powder. Stir well.
8. Add the red pepper sauce, stir, cover and cook over medium-low heat for about 45 minutes.
9. If sauce is too thick you may add water.
10. Serve and enjoy!

Yummy over rice!

2 lb. chicken pieces (thighs, breasts, legs)
2 tbsp. canola oil
1 cinnamon stick
1 bay leaf
1/4 tsp. fennel seeds
1/2 tsp. cumin seeds
1 c. onion, chopped
1/4 c. red pepper, chopped
6 cloves garlic, chopped
1 tbsp. ginger, minced
1/2 tsp. turmeric powder
2 tsp. curry powder
3/4 tsp. cayenne pepper
3/4 tsp. black pepper
3/4 tsp. cumin powder
1 c. roasted red pepper sauce

Percent Daily Values (DV) are based on a 2000 calorie diet

Calories	114.9	Protein	4.5g
Total Fats	9.3g	Potassium	85.8g
Sodium	37.1mg	Phosphorus	4.8%

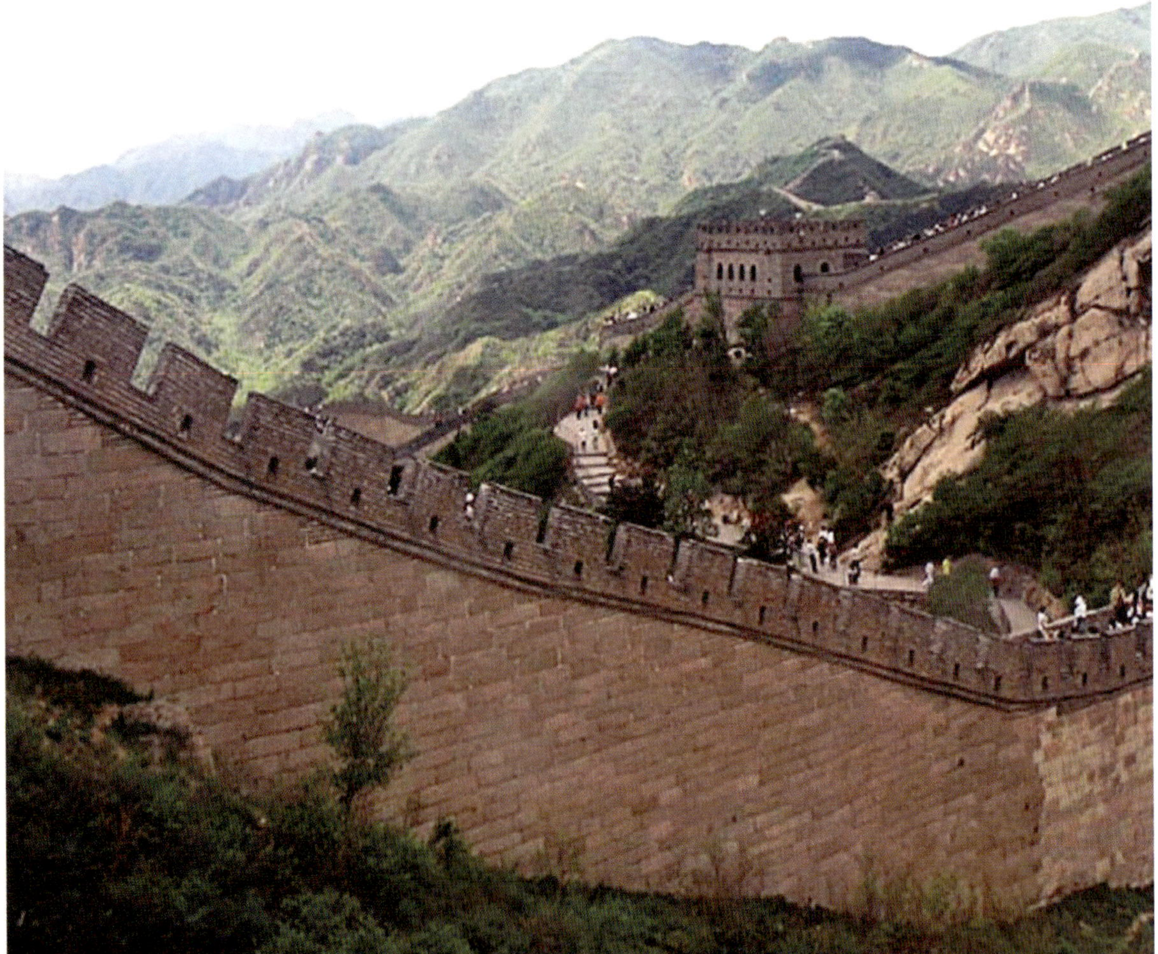

China

Chinese cooking is definitely an art. The two philosophies of Confucianism and Taoism influenced the way the Chinese cook and enjoy their dishes. Authentic Chinese food is typically very healthy and is enjoyed world round.

137 | Chinese Rousong

139 | Sesame Rice Balls

141 | Stir-Fry Chicken and Noodles

143 | Chinese Style Green Beans

145 | Puffed Pork Sung Bun

147 | Pineapple Coconut Bun

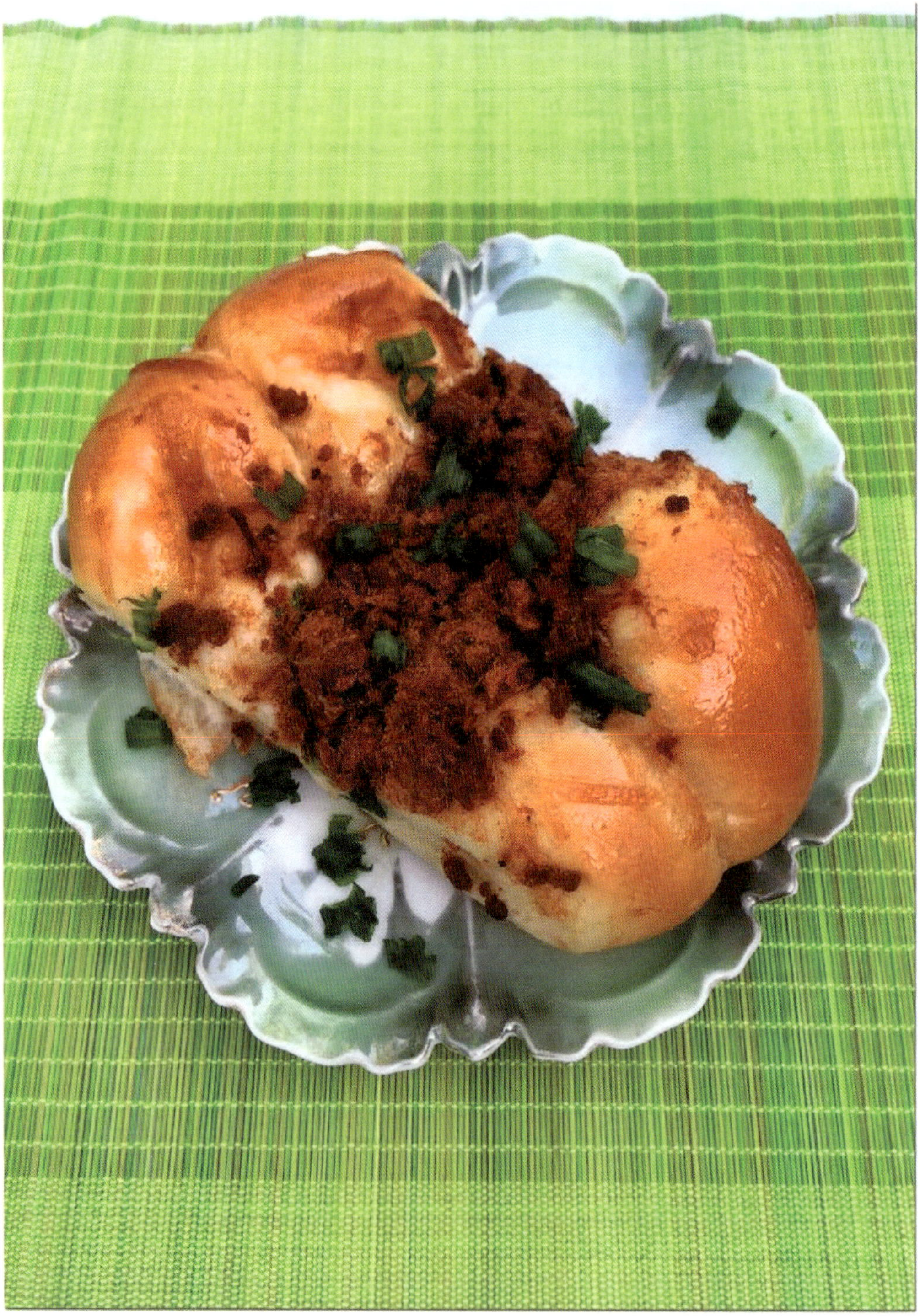

Chinese Rousong

Serves: 8
Prep Time: 10 min.
Cooking Time: 35 min.

1. Heat a wok or large skillet over medium-low.
2. Toss in the pork and stir for 30 minutes.
3. Remove from heat and shred the pork ultra-fine with forks.
4. In the same wok/skillet, add the soy sauce, sugar and pepper.
5. Stir for 30 seconds and add the pork back to the pan.
6. Cook, stirring constantly for 5 more minutes, or until the meat begins to crisp.
7. Serve on top of either a Chinese pastry or a brioche roll.
8. Garnish with scallions.

4 oz. lean pork, sliced thinly
1 tbsp. reduced-sodium soy sauce
1 tbsp. sugar
1 tsp. ground white pepper
scallions for garnish

Percent Daily Values (DV) are based on a 2000 calorie diet

Calories	26.9	Protein	7.1g
Total Fats	4.1g	Potassium	62.1g
Sodium	79.8mg	Phosphorus	3.7%

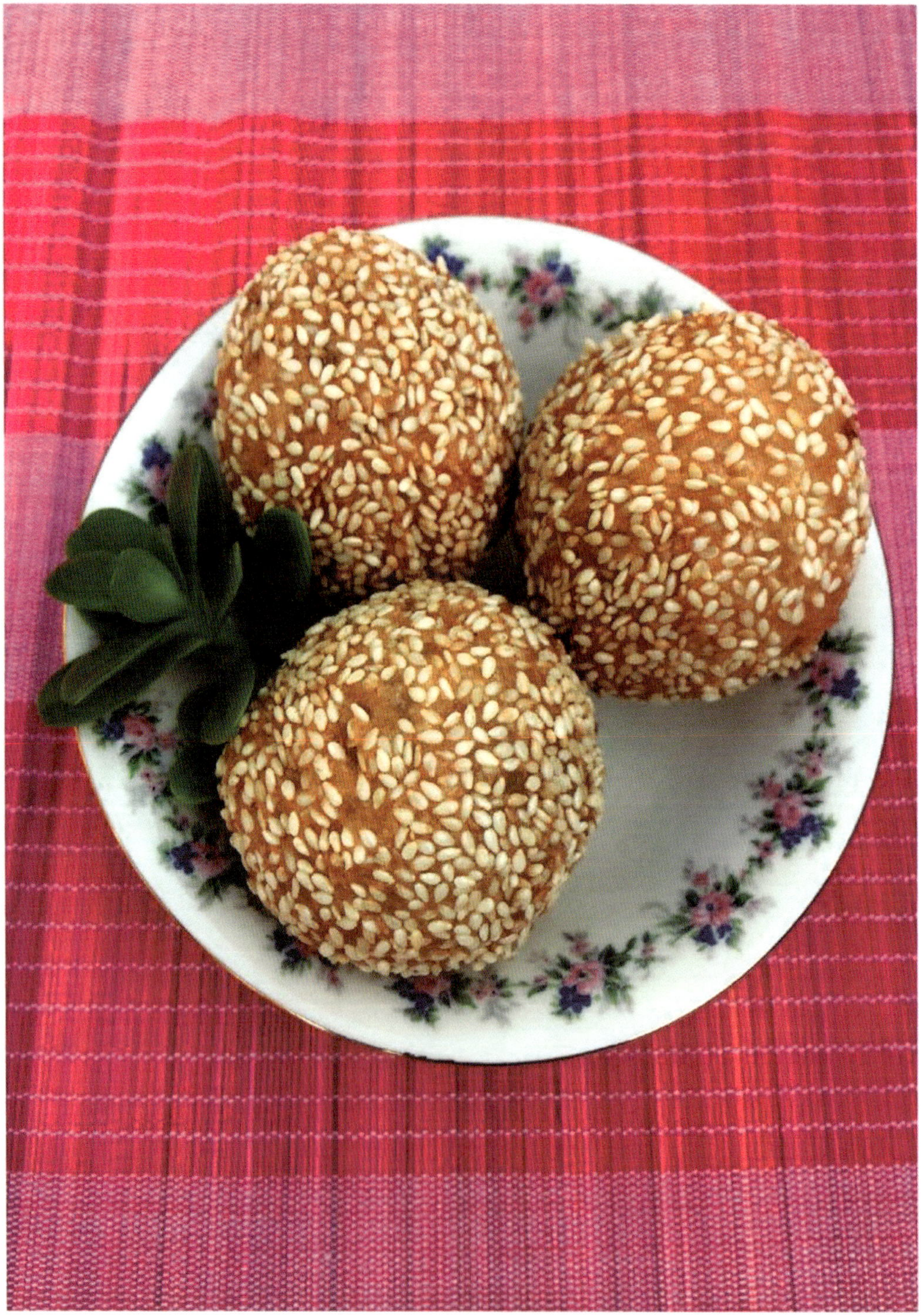

Sesame Rice Balls

Serves: 32
Prep Time: 30 min.
Cooking Time: 10 min.

1. Dissolve the sugar into 140ml hot water.
2. Add the sugar water to the flour and mix well.
3. Gather the dough into your hands and separate dough into 32 small balls.
4. Cook the balls in boiling water until floating.
5. Remove the balls and set aside, covered, for 10 minutes. This allows the flour to fully absorb the water added.
6. Dredge rice balls in white sesame seeds. If rice balls are dry, dunk quickly in water before dredging.
7. Press gently so sesame seeds stick well.
8. In a pot or wok, add oil to a depth of 4".
9. Heat until the oil is moderately hot, about 350°F.
10. Reduce heat to very low and add the rice balls. Cook in batches so they can move around freely.
11. Fry til the balls start floating and increase the heat to medium.
12. Stir gently to ensure even browning.
13. Cook the batches for 10 minutes, remove with a slotted spoon and drain on paper towels.

3 c. rice flour

6 tbsp. sugar

1/4 c. white sesame seeds, placed in a bowl for dredging

vegetable oil for frying

Percent Daily Values (DV) are based on a 2000 calorie diet

Calories	70.9	Protein	0.9g
Total Fats	1.1g	Potassium	11.3g
Sodium	0.0mg	Phosphorus	1.5%

139 | CHINA

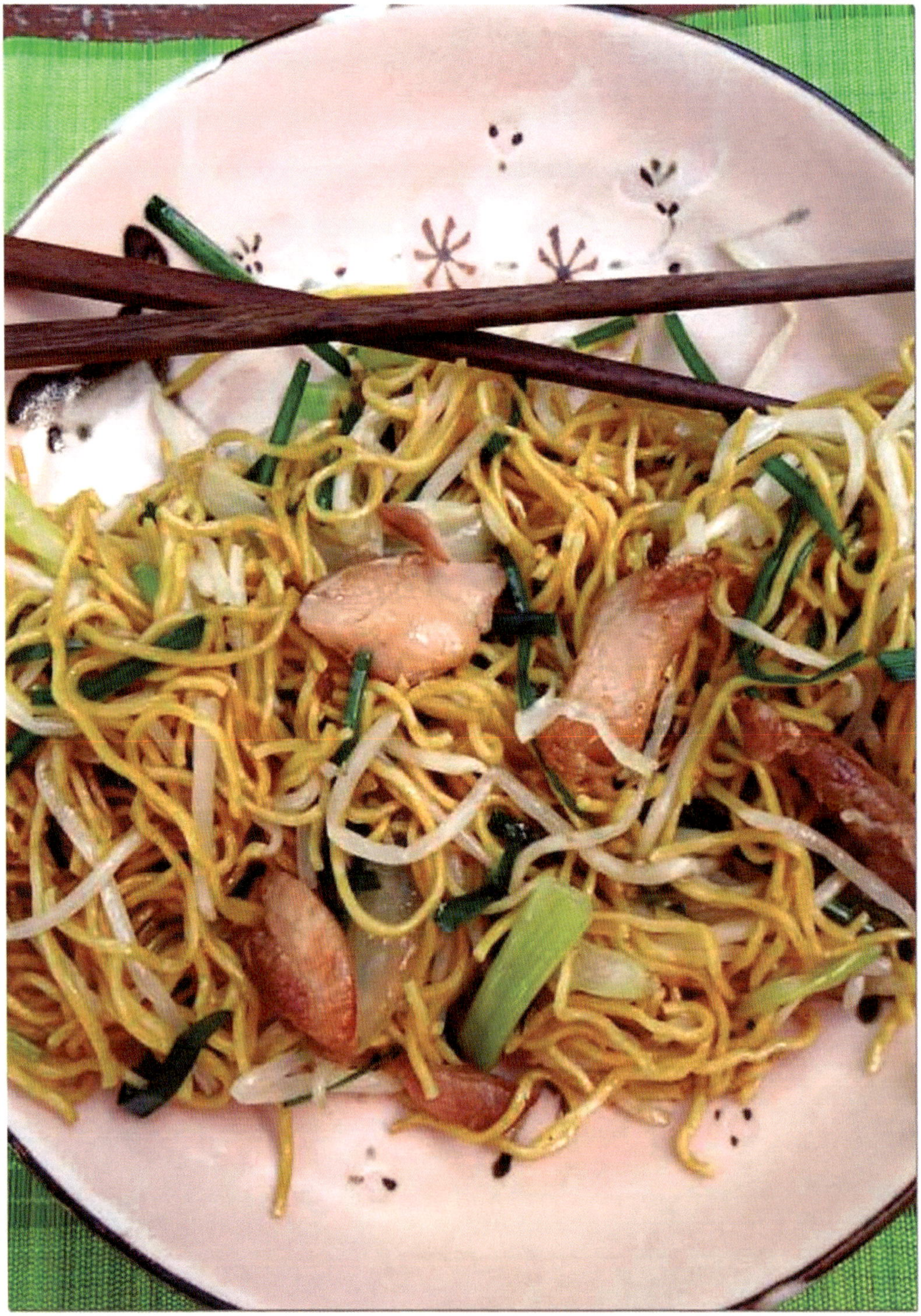

Stir-Fry Chicken and Noodles

Serves: 6
Prep Time: 20 min.
Cooking Time: 20 min.

1. Cook noodles according to package directions, omitting salt. Drain and set aside.
2. Slice the chicken thighs.
3. Heat olive oil in a wok or deep skillet over medium-high heat.
4. Add the chicken and sauté for 5 minutes or until no longer pink.
5. Add the onions, celery, and chili-garlic paste.
6. Stir-fry until the veggies are cooked but still crunchy, about 5 minutes.
7. Add noodles, bean sprouts and soy sauce, mix well and serve!

So easy and so good!

2 tbsp. olive oil
8 oz. rice noodles, cooked
1 lb. boneless skinless chicken thighs
1 c. green onions, sliced
1 c. celery, chopped
1 c. onion, chopped
1 tbsp. reduced-sodium soy sauce
1 tsp. chili-garlic paste
1/2 c. bean sprouts

Percent Daily Values (DV) are based on a 2000 calorie diet

Calories	218.8	Protein	19.5g
Total Fats	6.1g	Potassium	170.2g
Sodium	127.2mg	Phosphorus	7.0%

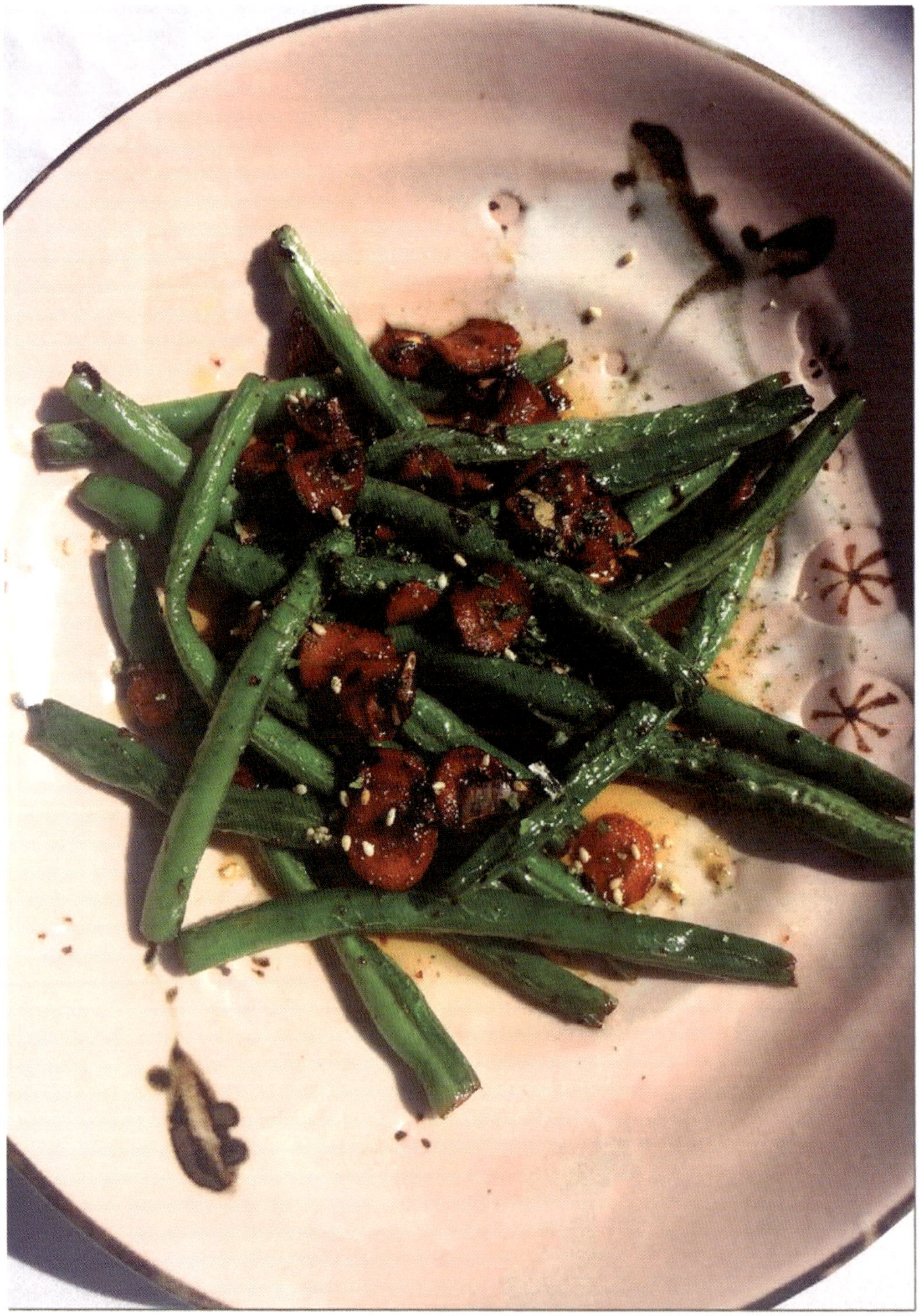

Chinese-Style Green Beans

Serves: 4
Prep Time: 10 min.
Cooking Time: 8 min.

1. Heat a wok or large skillet over high heat and add the oil.
2. Add the ginger and shallots and cook for 30 seconds.
3. Add the carrots, green beans and a splash of water and stir-fry for 5 minutes.
4. Add the soy sauce, vinegar and sesame oil and stir.
5. Remove from heat and place on a serving platter, and garnish with sesame seeds.

Chopsticks anyone?

1 tbsp. vegetable oil
1 tbsp. grated ginger
1 tbsp. shallots, chopped
1 carrot, peeled, sliced
1 1/2 c. green beans, trimmed
1 tbsp. reduced-sodium soy sauce
1 tsp. rice vinegar
1 tsp. toasted sesame oil
1 tsp. toasted sesame seeds

Percent Daily Values (DV) are based on a 2000 calorie diet

Calories	40.3	Protein	1.0g
Total Fats	2.3g	Potassium	120.5g
Sodium	150.2mg	Phosphorus	1.9%

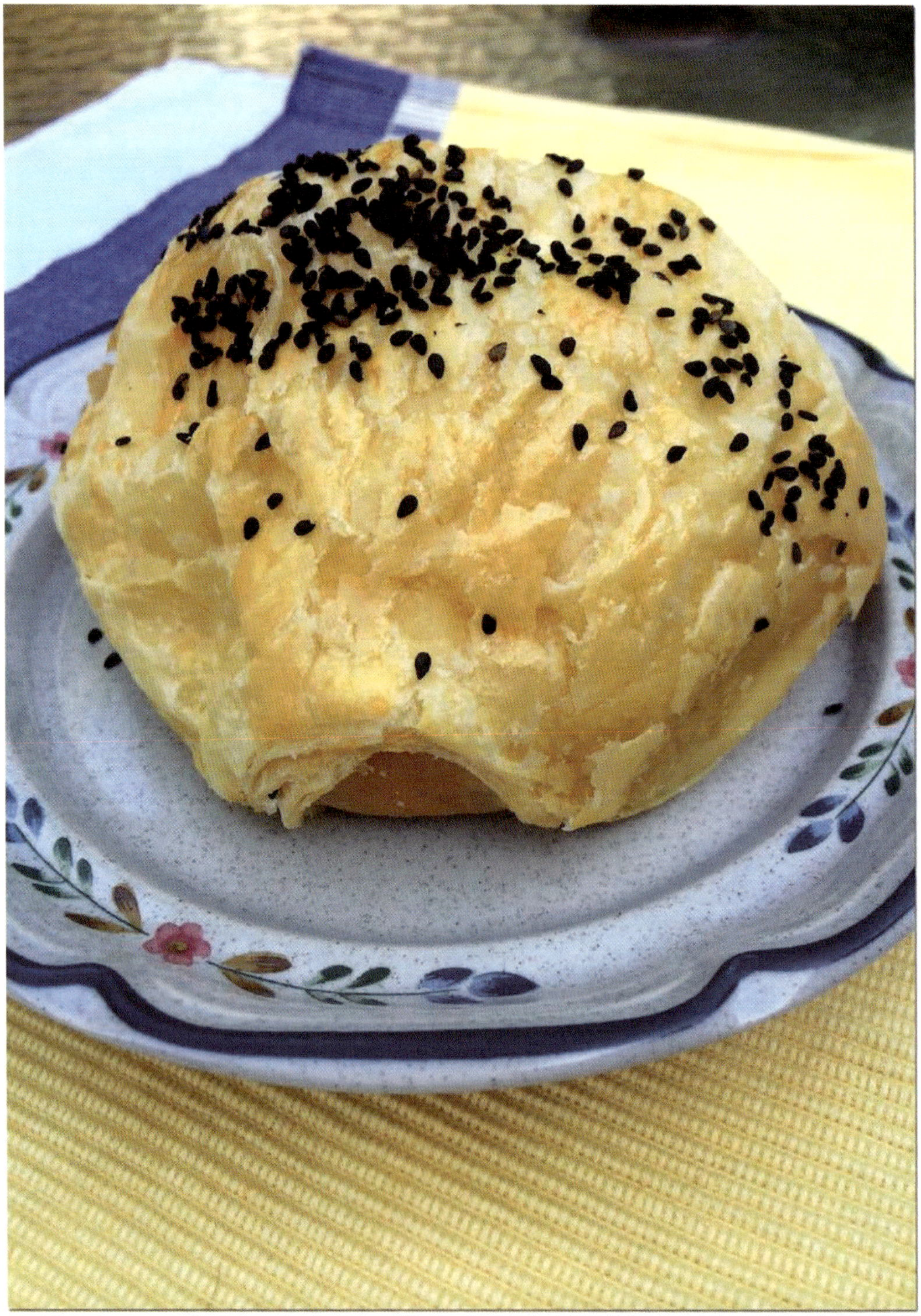

Puffed Pork Sung Bun

Serves: 12
Prep Time: 30 min.
Cooking Time: 30 min.

1. In a small bowl, mix together the warm water, sugar, yeast and let sit for 15 minutes.
2. In a large bowl, add the flour, egg, oil and the yeast mixture.
3. With your hands knead the dough for 2-3 minutes, adding flour if too sticky.
4. Place the dough in an oiled bowl and in a warm spot, let it rise until doubled in size.
5. In a medium-sized bowl, add the garlic-ginger paste, oil, honey, hoisin, soy sauce, 5 spice, sesame oil, and pepper.
6. Whisk together and add the ground pork.
7. Let the pork marinate for at least 1 hour.
8. Heat a large skillet over medium heat and add the vegetable oil.
9. Add the pork mixture and cook for 15 minutes.
10. Remove from heat and add the green onions, mix well.
11. Preheat the oven to 350°F.
12. Divide the dough into 12 equal pieces.
13. Using a rolling pin, roll each piece into a 4" x 5" disk.
14. Place a heaping tbsp. of the meat mixture into the middle of each disk.
15. Gather up the edges and pinch closed, sealing the bun.
16. Place the sealed side down on an ungreased baking sheet. Repeat.
17. Brush the buns with egg wash and bake for 20 minutes or until golden brown. Sprinkle with sesame seeds for garnish.

2 1/2 tsp. dried yeast
1/2 c. warm water
1/4 c. sugar
2 1/4 c. all-purpose flour
1 egg, beaten
3 tbsp. canola oil

Filling:

1 lb. extra-lean ground pork
2 tsp. garlic-ginger paste
1 tbsp. vegetable oil
2 tbsp. honey
2 tbsp. hoisin sauce
1 tbsp. reduced-sodium soy sauce
1/2 tsp. black pepper
1/2 tsp. 5 spice powder
1 tsp. sesame oil
1 tbsp. vegetable oil
2 green onions, chopped

1 egg, beaten (egg wash)
black sesame seeds for garnish

Percent Daily Values (DV) are based on a 2000 calorie diet

Calories	256.4	Protein	10.8g
Total Fats	13.0g	Potassium	155.0g
Sodium	80.9mg	Phosphorus	9.5%

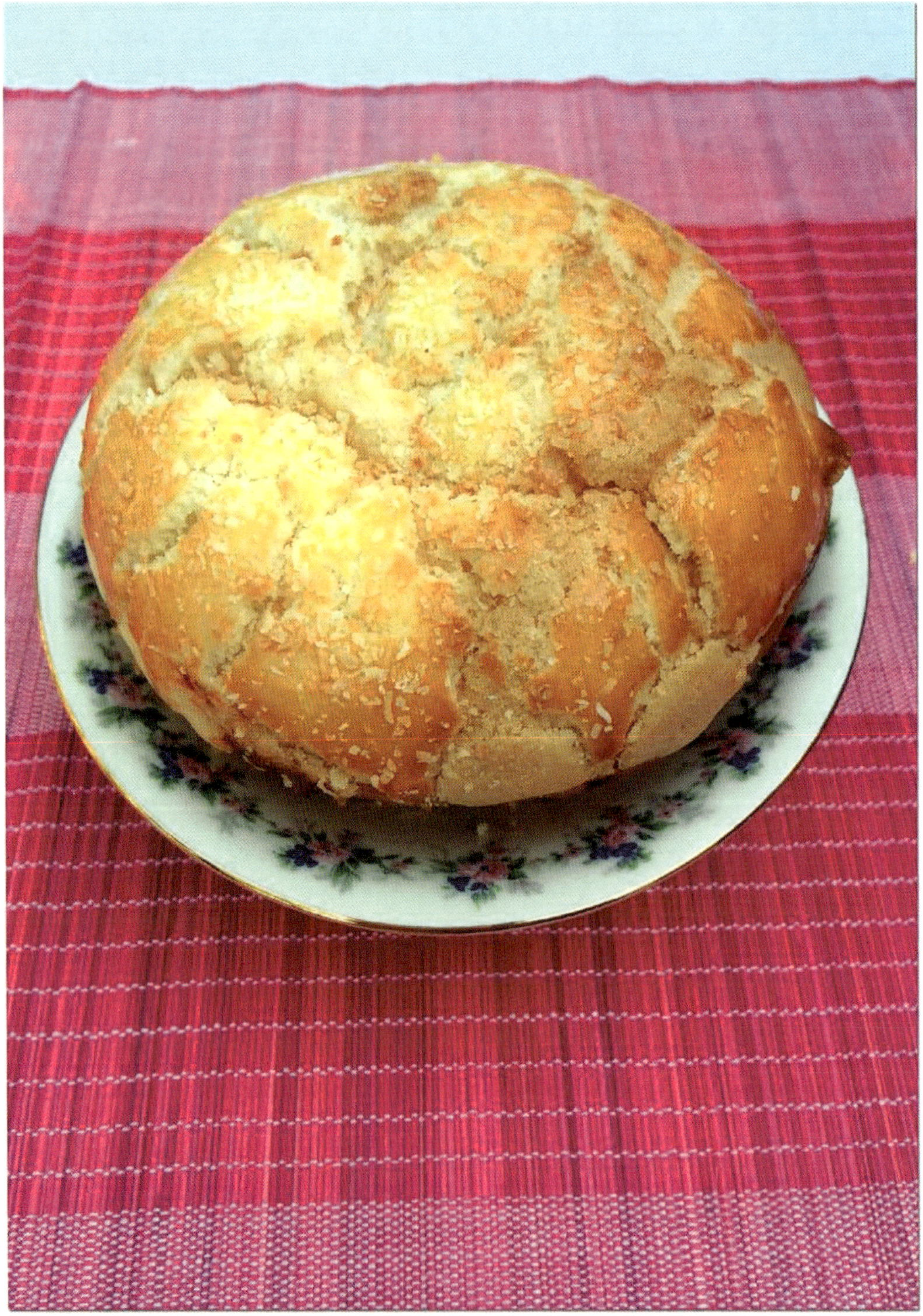

Pineapple Coconut Bun

Serves: 12
Prep Time: 3 hrs.
Cooking Time: 18 min.

1. Preheat oven to 350°F.
2. Blend together the coconut, pineapple and sugar until very smooth. Set aside.
3. To prepare the dough, combine the first 3 ingredients in a small bowl.
4. Let stand for 10 minutes.
5. In a large bowl, combine the next 4 ingredients, along with the egg and yeast mixture.
6. Slowly add the flour until a soft dough forms.
7. Cover with a towel, and let stand in a warm place for two hours until doubled in size.
8. Punch the dough down, cover and rest for 5 minutes.
9. Divide the dough into 12 portions.
10. With a rolling pin, roll each portion into a 5" x 3" shape.
11. Place a tbsp. of the coconut mixture in the center of each piece.
12. Bring all the sides up, pinching together to seal.
13. Place seam side down on a greased baking sheet, brush with the eggwash.
14. Bake for 18 minutes or until golden brown.
15. Remove from the oven and brush with the honey wash.

2 c. coconut flakes
1 c. pineapple chunks
2 tbsp. sugar
4 tbsp. melted light margarine
2 egg yolks

Dough:
1/3 c. warm water
1 tsp. sugar
2 tsp. active dry yeast
1/3 c. sugar
cooking spray
1/4 c. boiling water
1 egg, beaten
2 1/4 c. all-purpose flour

Egg Wash:
2 eggs, beaten
2 tbsp. water

Honey Wash:
2 tbsp. honey
2 tbsp. water

Percent Daily Values (DV) are based on a 2000 calorie diet

Calories	363.7	Protein	6.9g
Total Fats	12.5g	Potassium	74.5g
Sodium	122.4mg	Phosphorus	3.0%

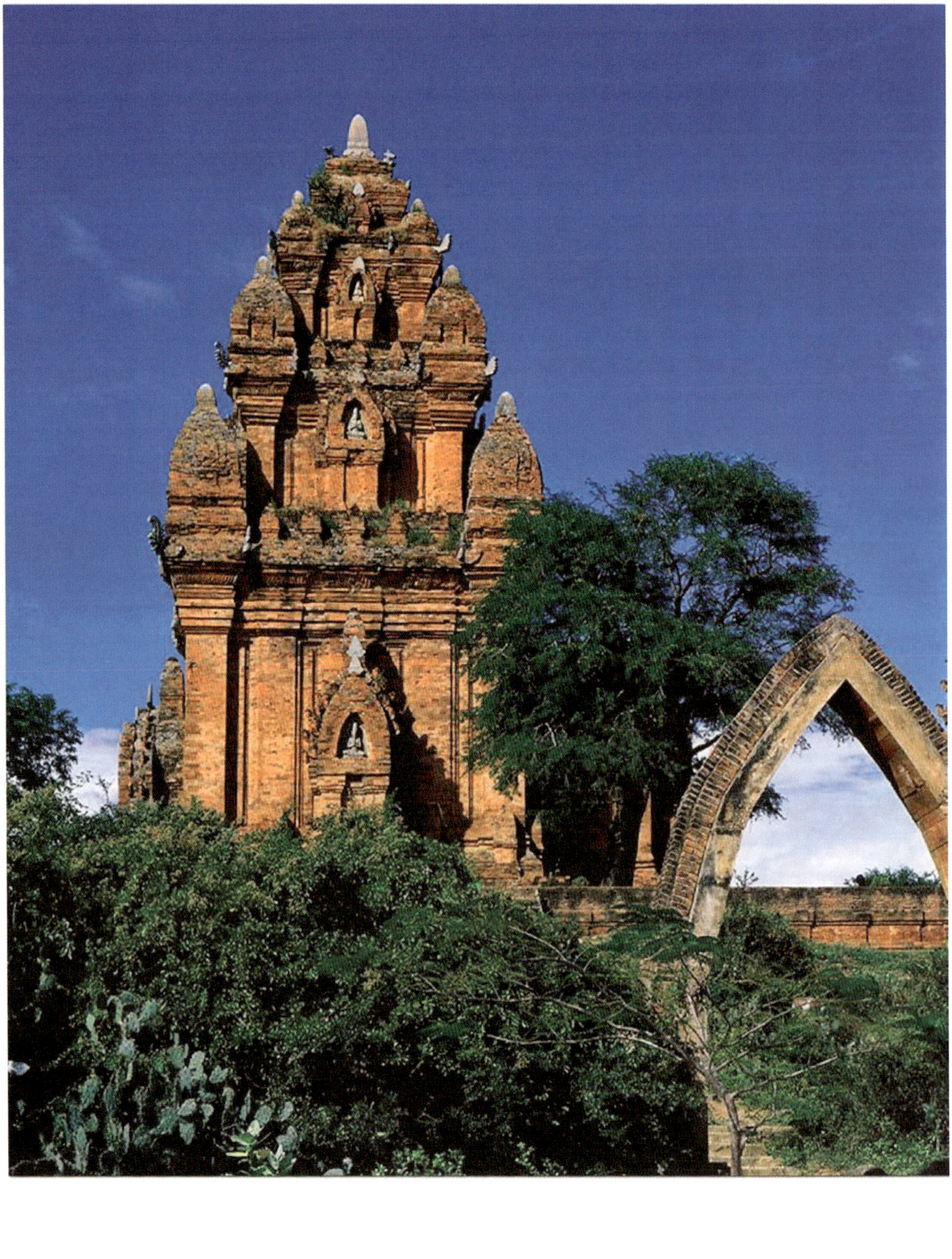

Vietnam

Vietnamese cooking is known around the world for its ingenious uses of fresh herbs, produce, spices, meats and fish, making it one of the healthiest cuisines in the world.
Also known for its culinary balance of five elements ... the spicy (metal), sour (wood), bitter (fire), salty (water) and sweet (Earth) are all encompassed in their food.

151 | Coconut Custard French Bread
153 | Nem Nuong Meatballs
155 | Vietnamese Spring Rolls 3 Ways
157 | Vietnamese Larb
159 | Savory Vietnamese Tilapia

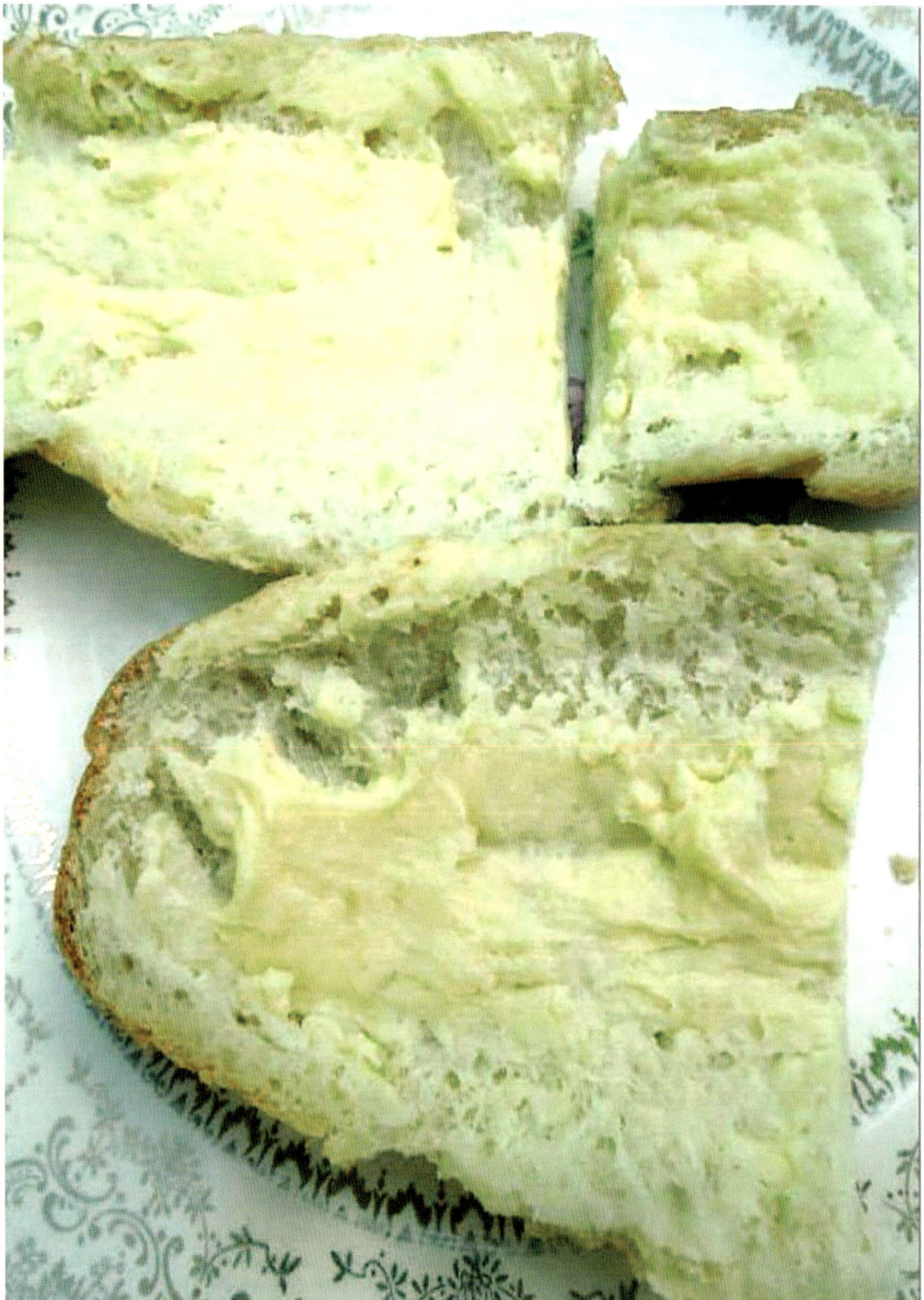

Coconut Custard French Bread

Serves: 6
Prep Time: 10 min.
Cooking Time: 20 min.

1. Beat the eggs, sugar, milk and vanilla until frothy.
2. Pour the liquid into a double-broiler and cook for 20 minutes, stirring frequently.
3. Remove from heat and pour the custard into a bowl and let cool.
4. When the custard is cooled, place in the refrigerator and let chill until set.
5. To serve, spread the custard onto the sliced French bread for a little taste of heaven!

So delicious!

5 eggs
1 c. coconut milk
1 c. sugar
1 tsp. vanilla
6 slices French bread

Percent Daily Values (DV) are based on a 2000 calorie diet

Calories	290.0	Protein	8.2g
Total Fats	5.8g	Potassium	88.4g
Sodium	180.0mg	Phosphorus	8.7%

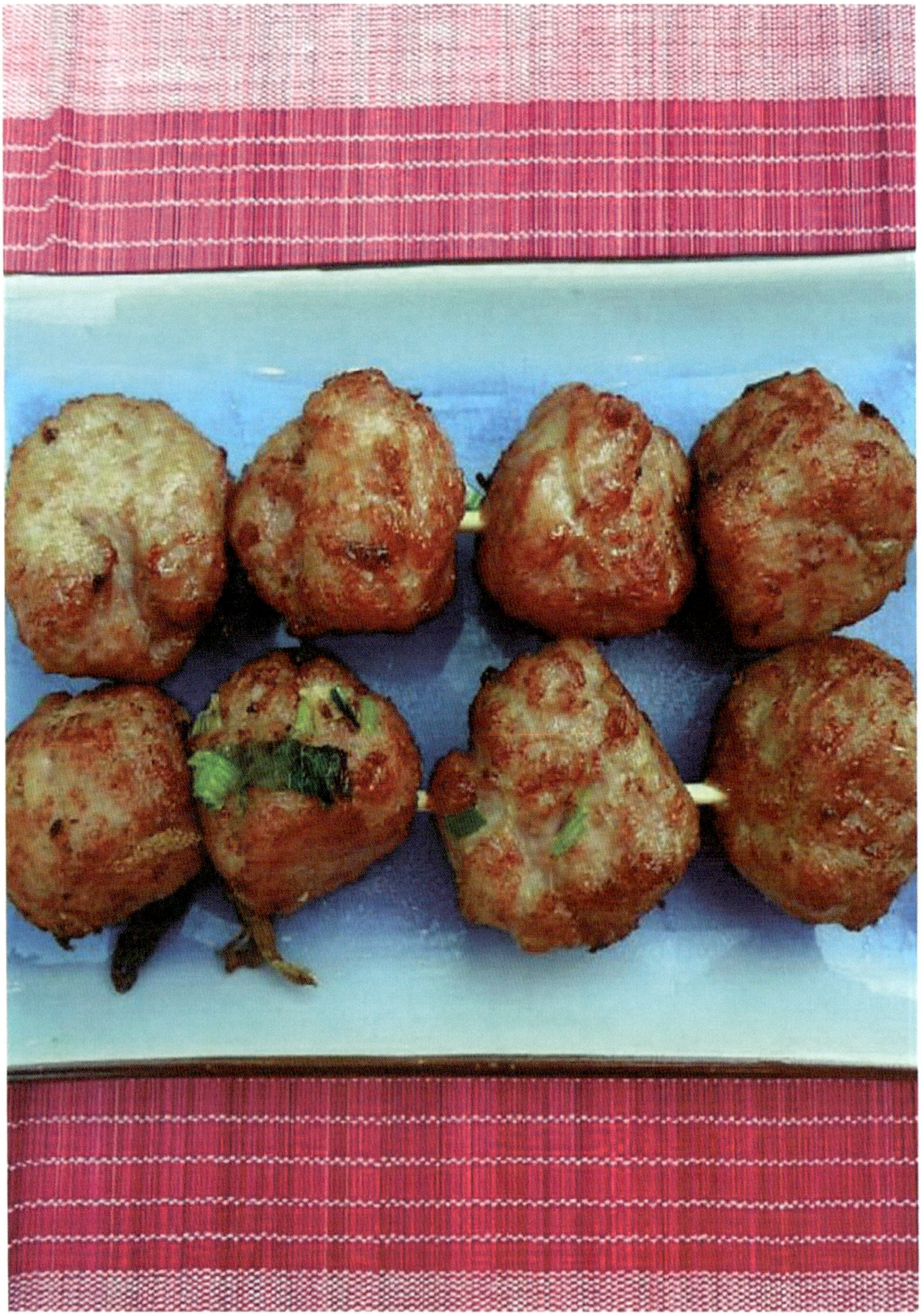

Nem Nuong Meatballs

Serves: 8
Prep Time: 30 min.
Cooking Time: 1 hr.

1. In a large bowl, combine the pork, shallots, garlic, sugar, soy-sauce and pepper.
2. Mix to combine well.
3. Cover and refrigerate for 1 hour or overnight.
4. Place the rice in a small skillet over medium-high heat, stirring constantly, until the rice is toasted golden brown.
5. Let the rice cool.
6. Place toasted rice in a grinder and process until it is a fine powder.
7. Remove the meat mixture from the refrigerator, place in a food processor and process to a stiff paste.
8. Add the oil and 3 tbsp. of the toasted rice and pulse just enough to combine.
9. Transfer the mixture to a bowl.
10. Divide the meat mixture into 1 1/2 tbsp. balls.
11. Thread the meatballs onto the skewers and grill on a grill pan for 30 minutes, turning occasionally.

1 1/2 lbs. lean ground pork
1/2 c. shallots, finely chopped
3 tbsp. minced garlic
4 tsp. sugar
1 tbsp. low-sodium soy sauce
1 tbsp. black pepper
5 tbsp. sushi rice
1 tbsp. canola oil
soaked skewers

Percent Daily Values (DV) are based on a 2000 calorie diet

Calories	282.5	Protein	12.3g
Total Fats	12.3g	Potassium	163.9g
Sodium	120.7mg	Phosphorus	8.5%

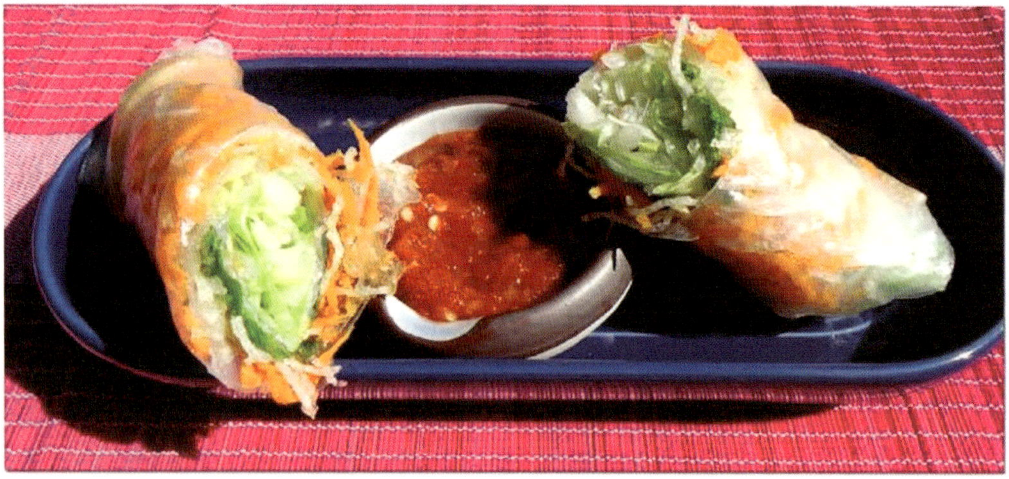

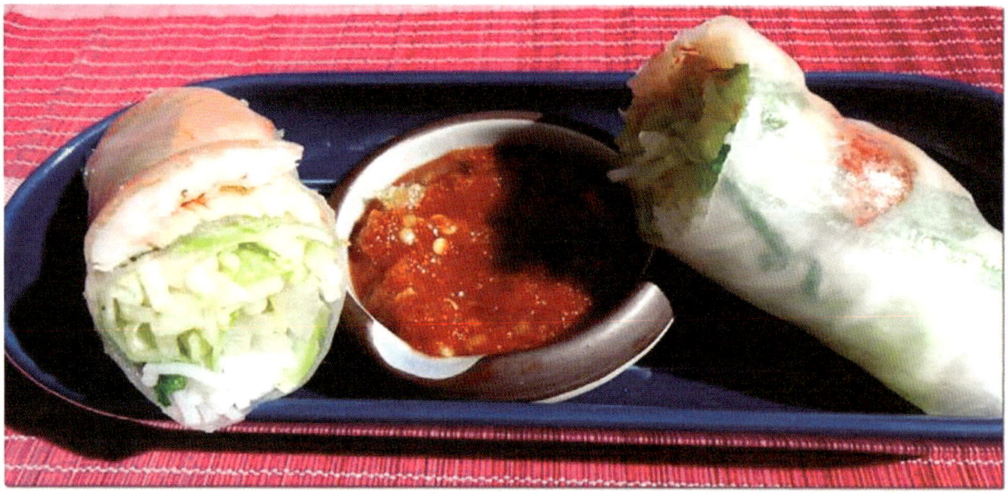

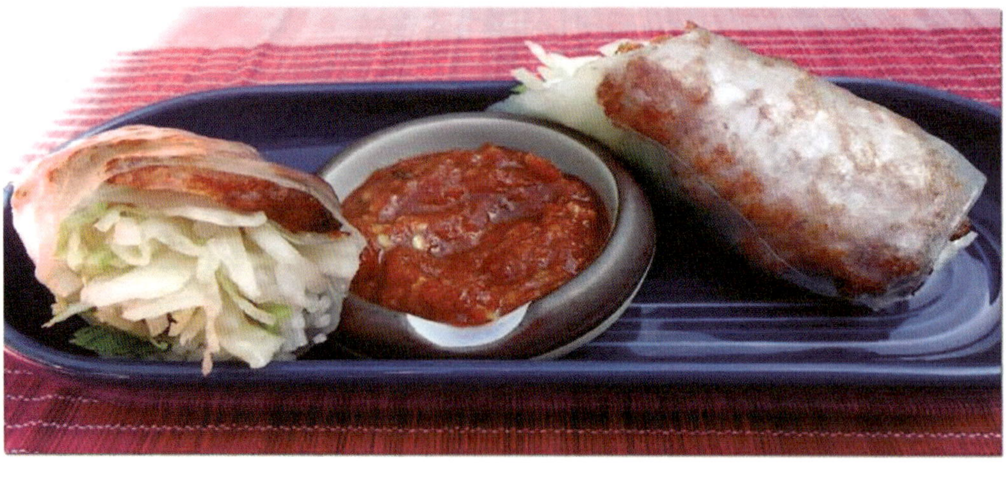

Vietnamese Spring Rolls 3 Ways

Serves: 30
Prep Time: 30 min.
Cooking Time: 40 min.

1. Preheat oven to 375°F.
2. In a small bowl, combine the soy sauce, garlic and honey.
3. In a roasting pan, place the pork tenderloin.
4. Pour the soy sauce marinade over the meat and turn to coat.
5. Roast for 40 minutes or until pork is thoroughly cooked.
6. When cool, slice into 1 1/2" long strips and set aside.
7. Poach the shrimp in boiling water until pink. Set aside.
8. In a large bowl, toss together the vermicelli, carrots, mint and cilantro.
9. Fill a bowl with hot water, dip one rice paper into water and place on a dishtowel.
10. Arrange the lettuce leaf on the wrapper, then spoon 2 tbsp. of the vermicelli filling onto the lettuce.
11. At this point choose the pork or shrimp as your additional filling.
12. Fold the bottom edge over the filling and tuck in the sides.

1 lb. pork tenderloin, trimmed

1 1/2 lbs. medium shrimp

2 tbsp. honey

2 tbsp. garlic, minced

1 tbsp. low-sodium soy sauce

1/2 lb. rice vermicelli, cooked

1 c. romaine lettuce

2 carrots, peeled, shredded

handful fresh mint leaves, chopped

3/4 c. fresh cilantro, chopped

30 round rice paper wrappers

*** Nutritional information is based on this recipe with all the ingredients added.

Percent Daily Values (DV) are based on a 2000 calorie diet

Calories	110.0	Protein	8.3g
Total Fats	1.5g	Potassium	89.4g
Sodium	83.7mg	Phosphorus	7.8%

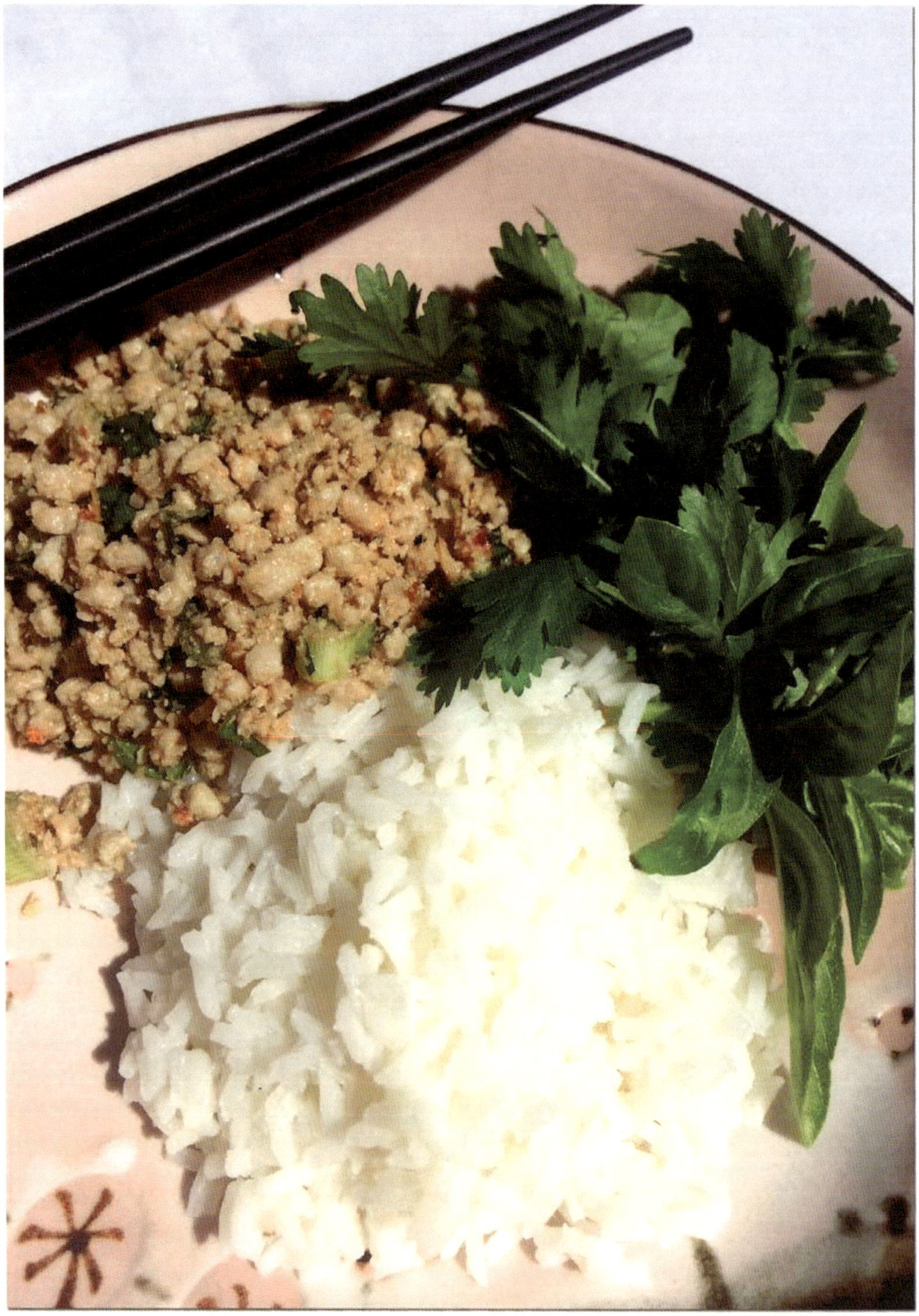

Vietnamese Larb

Serves: 6
Prep Time: 30 min.
Cooking Time: 30 min.

1. Preheat the oven to 350°F.
2. Spread the rice onto a baking sheet.
3. Bake the rice for 15 minutes.
4. Remove from oven and let cool.
5. Put the rice in a spice grinder and grind into a fine powder. Set aside.
6. In a large skillet, heat the oil over medium heat.
7. Stir in the garlic, galangal, peppers, and green onions.
8. Sauté for 3 minutes.
9. Add the ground pork, stirring constantly to break up lumps and sauté for 5 more minutes.
10. Stir in the worcestershire, shrimp paste and sugar.
11. Reduce the heat to simmer and cook for 5 minutes more until all the liquid has evaporated.
12. Remove from heat and stir in the ground rice, mint, basil and lime juice.
13. Serve with rice or lettuce cups if desired.

1/4 c. uncooked long-grain white rice
2 lbs. lean ground pork
2 tbsp. canola oil
4 garlic cloves, minced
2 tbsp. minced galangal
2 small red chili peppers, chopped
4 green onions, chopped
1 tsp. worcestershire sauce
1 tbsp. shrimp paste
1 tbsp. white sugar
3 tbsp. fresh mint, chopped
2 tbsp. fresh basil, chopped
1/4 c. lime juice

Percent Daily Values (DV) are based on a 2000 calorie diet

Calories	217.7	Protein	14.2g
Total Fats	10.6g	Potassium	250.3g
Sodium	42.1mg	Phosphorus	10.4%

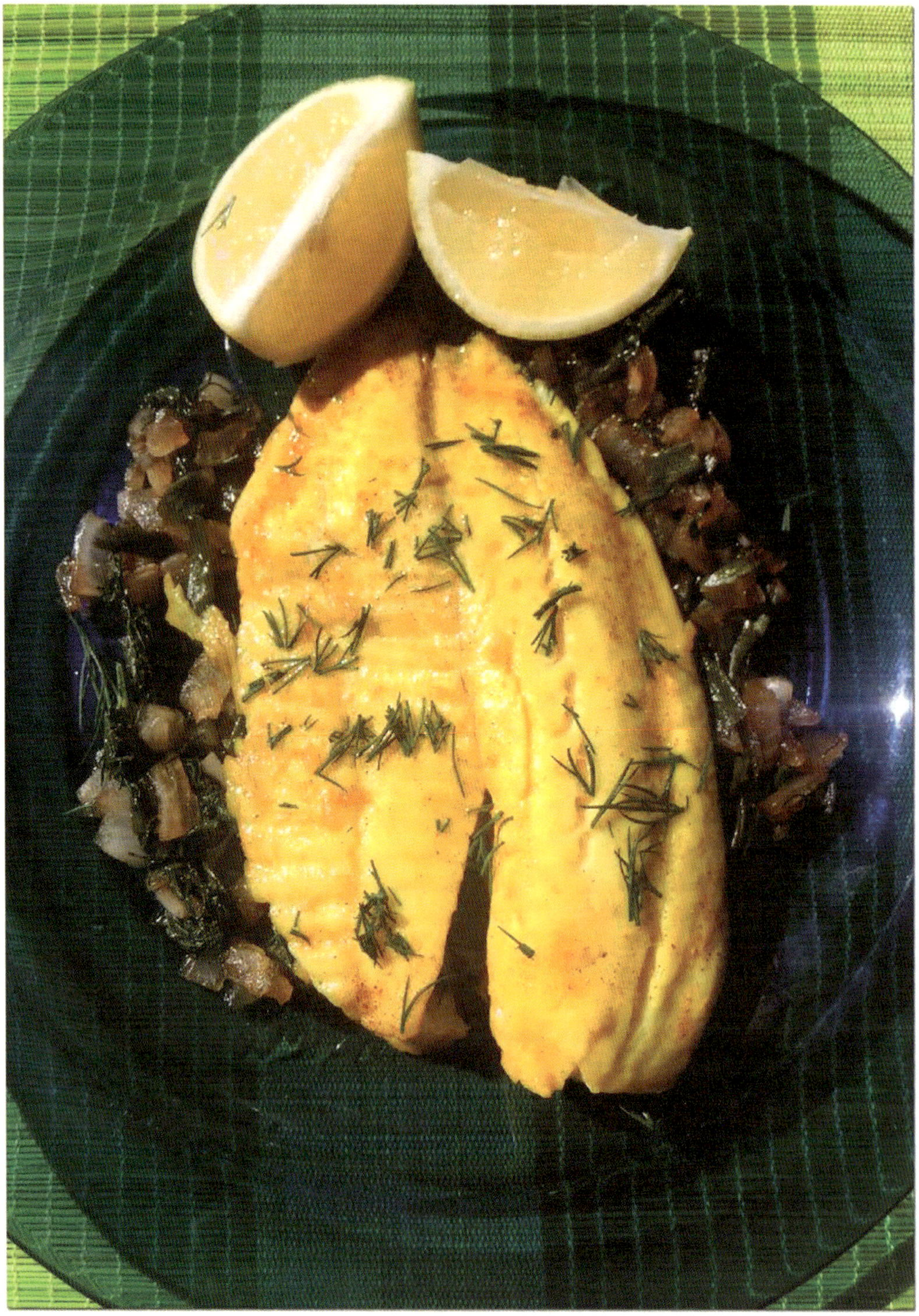

Savory Vietnamese Tilapia

Serves: 4
Prep Time: 20 min.
Cooking Time: 10 min.

1. Combine the first 8 ingredients in a large bowl, stirring with a whisk until smooth.
2. Add the fish, cover and chill for 2 hours.
3. Heat a large skillet over high heat, coating with cooking spray.
4. Add the onion, 1/4 c. dill and green onions.
5. Stir-fry for 3 minutes.
6. Add the soy sauce and sugar, and stir-fry for one more minute.
7. Arrange the onion mixture on a platter, set aside.
8. In the same skillet, add the fish.
9. Cook for 3 minutes, turn the fish over and cook 2 more minutes, or until the fish flakes easily with a fork.
10. Place the fish on the platter over the onion mixture.
11. Sprinkle with 1/4 c. dill, and serve with the lemon wedges.

1/4 c. shallots, sliced
1 tbsp. fresh dill, chopped
1 tbsp. minced garlic
1 tbsp. ginger, grated
1 tbsp. worcestershire sauce
1 tbsp. sesame oil
1 tsp. ground turmeric
1 tsp. black pepper
4 tilapia filets, each cut into 4 pieces
cooking spray
2 c. yellow onion, sliced
4 scallions, sliced
1 tbsp. reduced-sodium soy sauce
2 tsp. white sugar
lemon wedges for garnish

Percent Daily Values (DV) are based on a 2000 calorie diet

Calories	211.3	Protein	13.1g
Total Fats	10.2g	Potassium	302.2g
Sodium	201.1mg	Phosphorus	4.3%

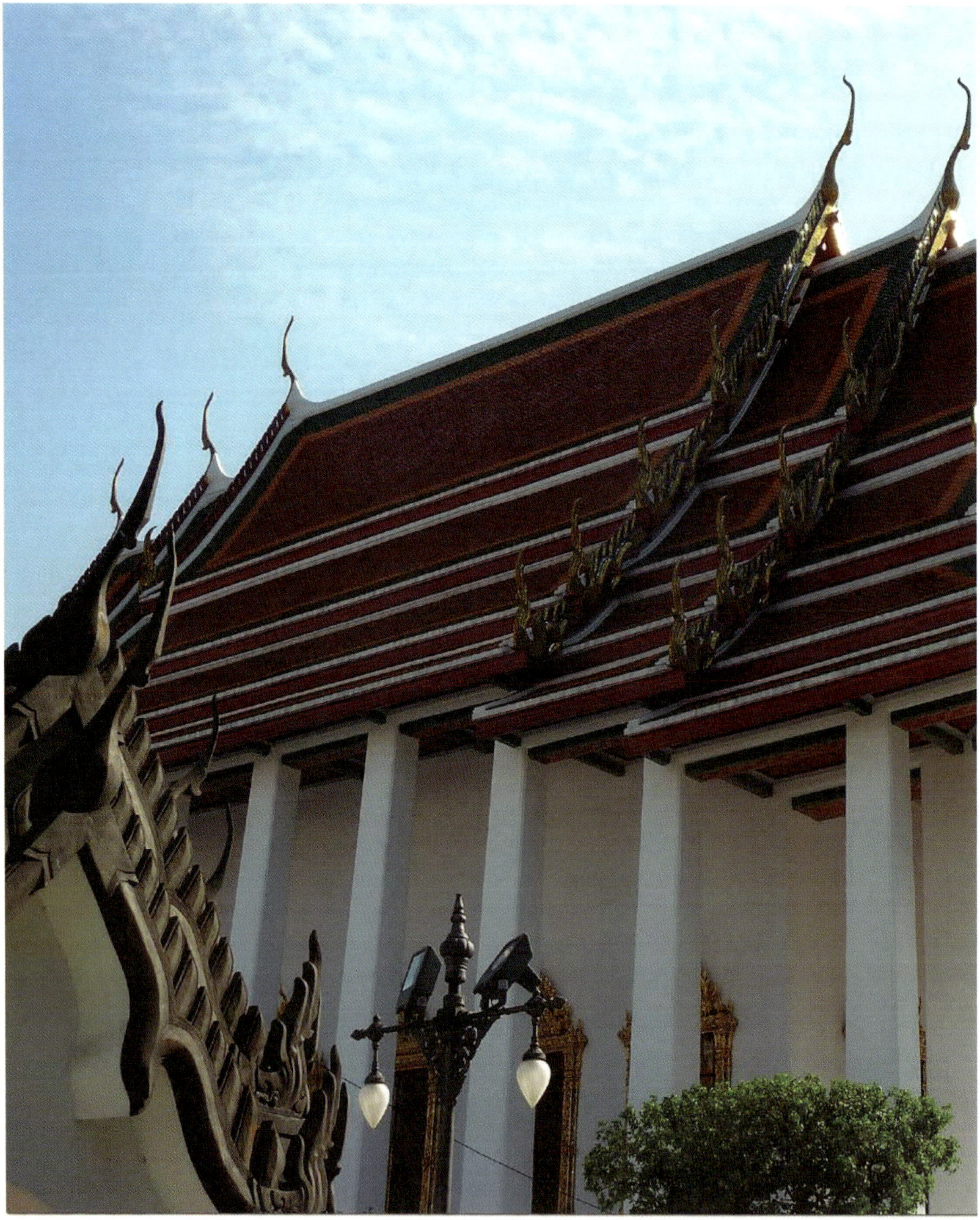

Thailand

Thailand was a crossroads of East to West sea routes, causing it's culture and food to be influenced by many countries including India and China.

163 | Spicy Thai Pork Salad

165 | Thai Onion Cakes

167 | Chopped Thai Salad

169 | Khao Mok Gai

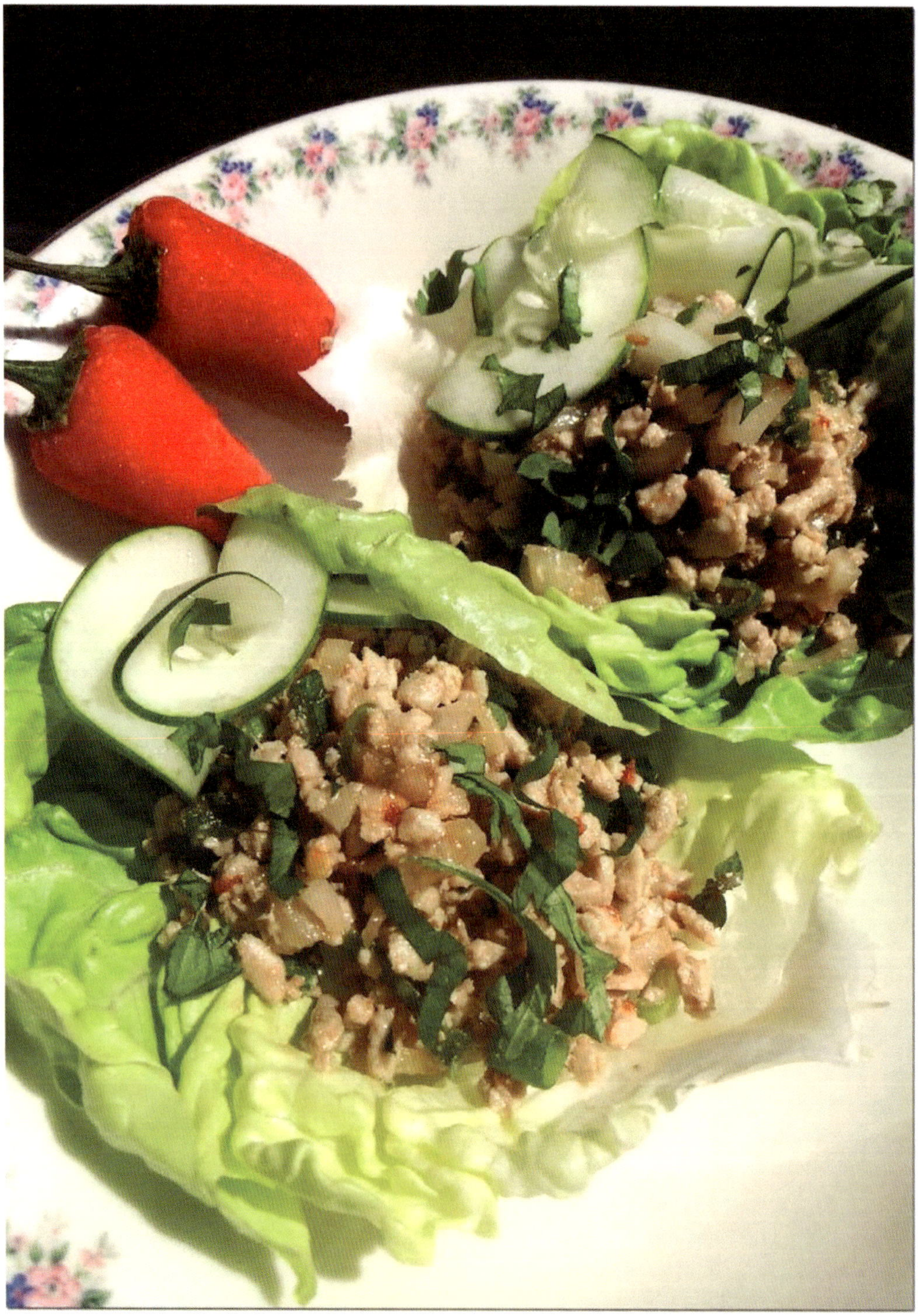

Spicy Thai Pork Salad

Serves: 8
Prep Time: 15 min.
Cooking Time: 7 min.

1. Heat a large skillet over medium-high heat.
2. Cook the pork with 1/4 of the shallots, and 1 tbsp. lime juice, for 7 minutes stirring constantly to separate any lumps.
3. In a large bowl, combine remaining shallots, lime juice, scallions, worcestershire sauce, chili sauce, mint and cilantro.
4. Add the pork mixture and toss well to coat.
5. To serve, place a lettuce leaf on a plate and top with pork mixture and cucumber slices.

Great for lunch!

- 1 lb. lean ground pork
- 4 shallots, sliced
- 2 tbsp. fresh lime juice
- 2 scallions, sliced
- 1 tsp. worcestershire sauce
- 1 tsp. Thai chili sauce
- 1/4 c. fresh mint leaves, chopped
- 1/4 c. fresh cilantro leaves, chopped
- 8 leaves butter lettuce
- 1 cucumber, thinly sliced

Percent Daily Values (DV) are based on a 2000 calorie diet

Calories	125.3	Protein	10.4g
Total Fats	8.2g	Potassium	184.3g
Sodium	43.8mg	Phosphorus	9.5%

163 | THAILAND

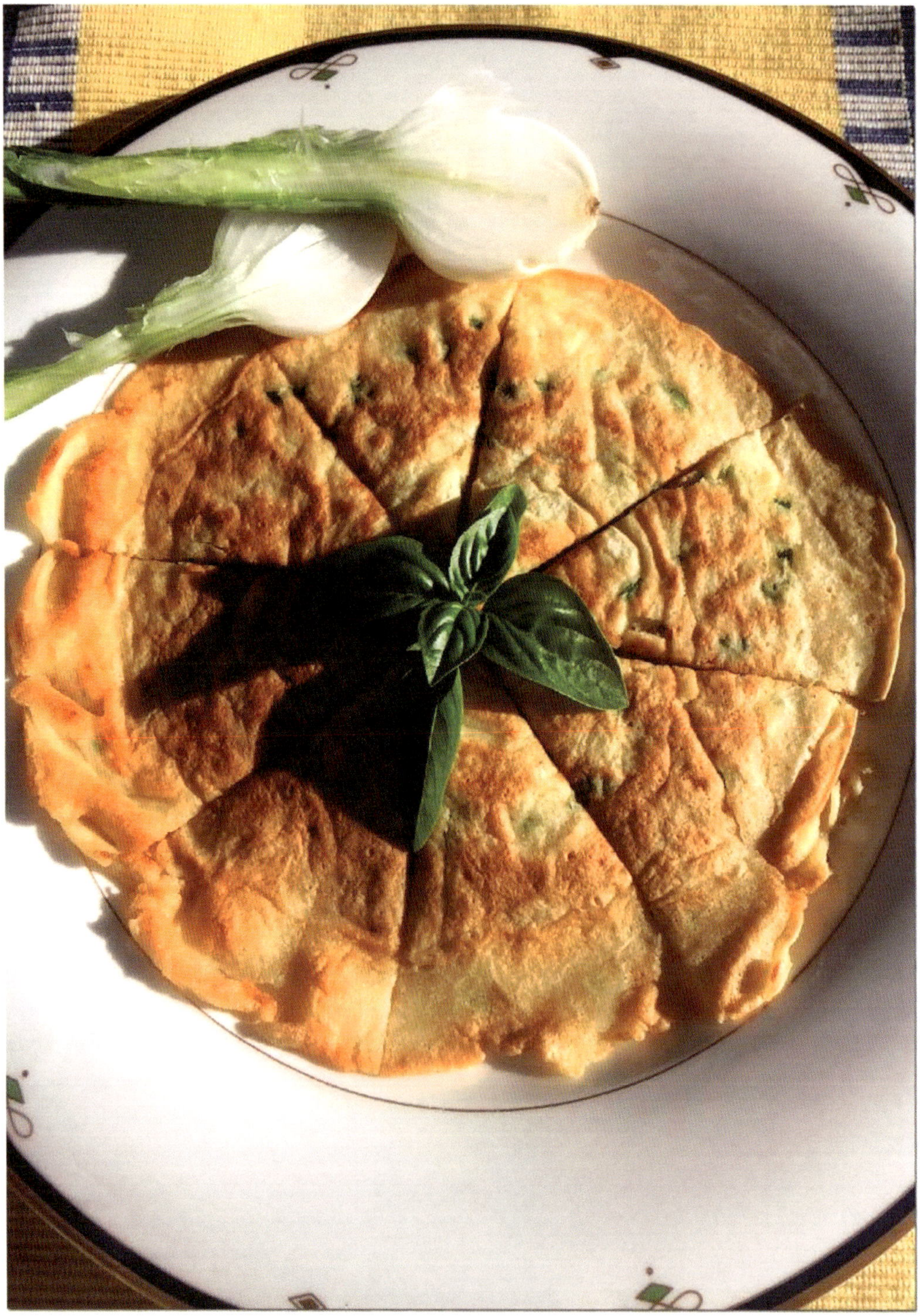

Thai Onion Cakes

Serves: 8
Prep Time: 10 min.
Cooking Time: 12 min.

1. In a large bowl, stir together all the ingredients.
2. In a large skillet, heat the oil over medium-high heat.
3. Pour batter into the skillet to make one large pancake.
4. Cook for 12 minutes or until golden brown, turning once.
5. Remove from skillet, and cut into 8 wedges.

So yummy!

- 1/2 c. all-purpose flour
- 1/2 bunch scallions, chopped
- 1 tsp. ground ginger
- 1/2 tsp. baking soda
- 1 tsp. cream of tartar
- 1/2 tsp. cumin
- 1 tbsp. chopped basil
- 1/2 c. water
- 1 egg, lightly beaten
- 2 tsp. olive oil
- dash of red pepper flakes

Percent Daily Values (DV) are based on a 2000 calorie diet

Calories	41.4	Protein	1.8g
Total Fats	0.8g	Potassium	78.1g
Sodium	75.4mg	Phosphorus	2.4%

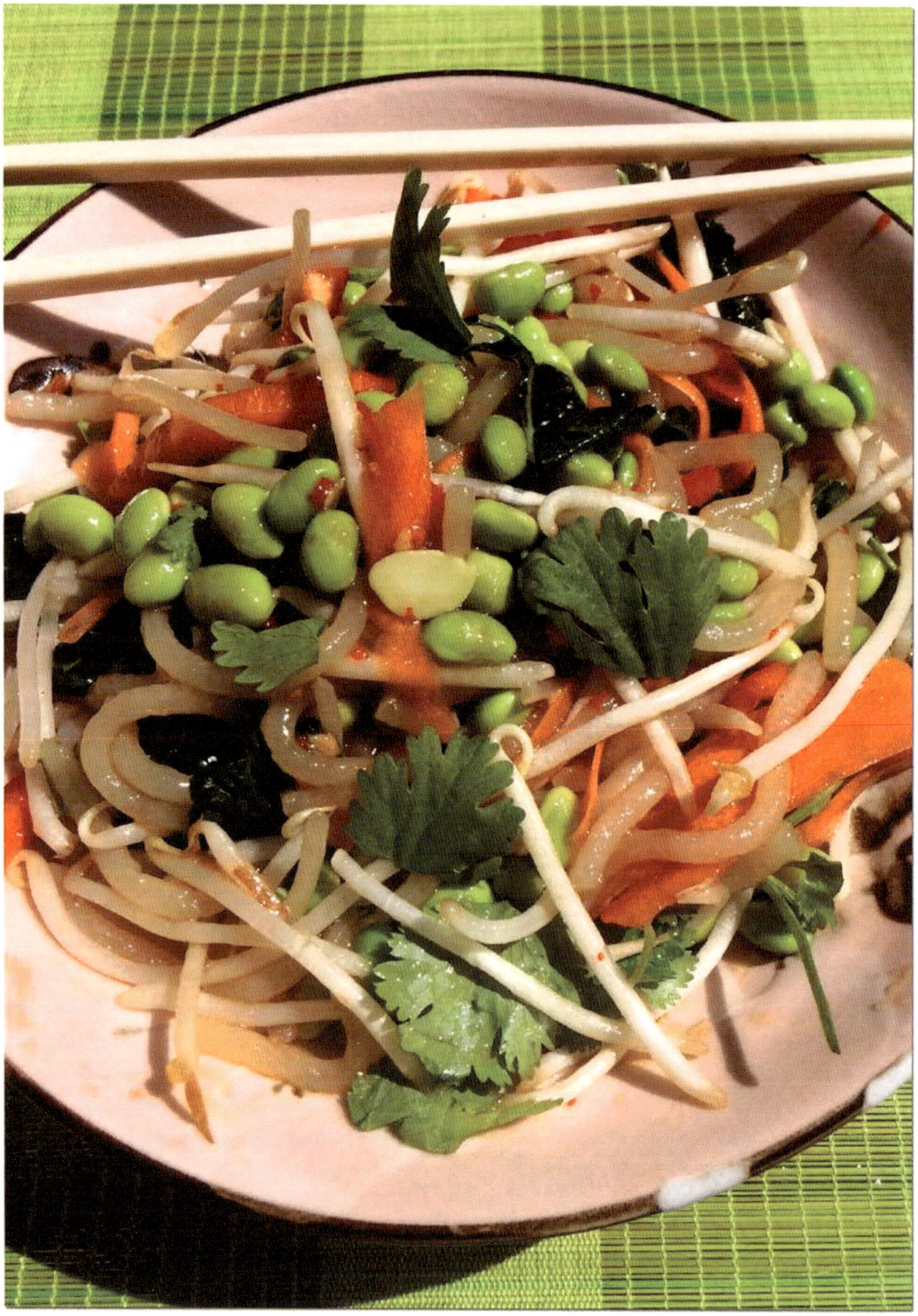

Chopped Thai Salad

Serves: 6
Prep Time: 20 min.
Cooking Time: 5 min.

1. Puree all the dressing ingredients in a food processor until smooth.
2. Cook the edamame in a pot of boiling water for 3 minutes. Drain and allow to cool.
3. Slice up the kale, carrots, peppers, green onions and cilantro leaves into thin strips.
4. In a large bowl, toss all the vegetables and rice noodles together and drizzle with the dressing.
5. Toss gently and serve immediately.

Crunchy and delicious!

Dressing:
3 tbsp. canola oil
1 thai chili, chopped
3 cloves garlic, chopped
2 tbsp. low-sodium soy sauce
2 tbsp. water
1 tbsp. white vinegar
1 tbsp. honey
1 tbsp. sesame oil
1 tbsp. ginger

Salad:
1/2 c. frozen shelled edamame
3 c. baby kale
1 c. rice noodles, cooked
3 carrots
2 bell peppers
1/2 c. bean sprouts
1/2 c. cilantro leaves
2 green onions

Percent Daily Values (DV) are based on a 2000 calorie diet

Calories	87.3	Protein	3.4g
Total Fats	3.3g	Potassium	204.9g
Sodium	31.4mg	Phosphorus	2.9%

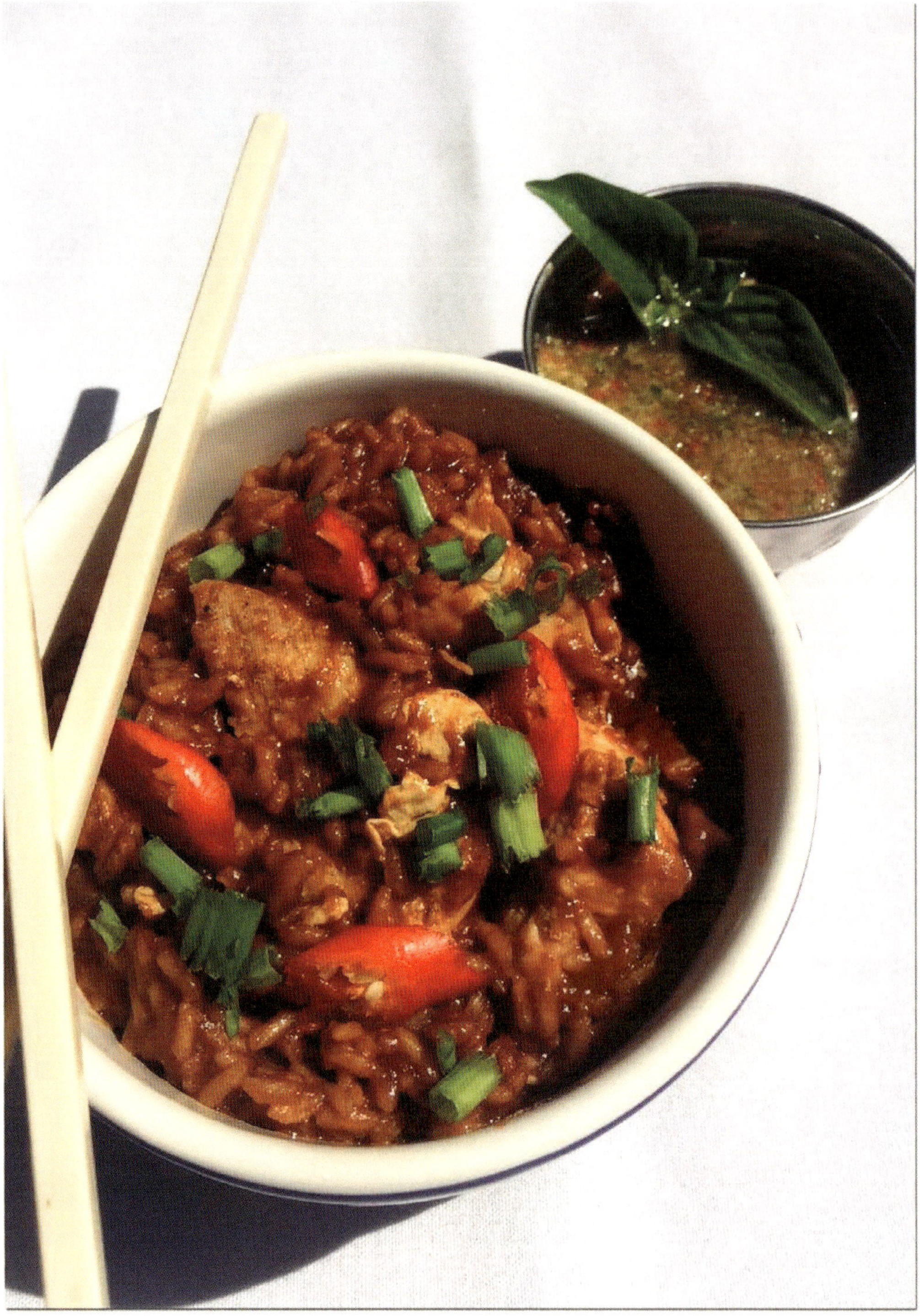

Khao Mok Gai

Serves: 8
Prep Time: 20 min.
Cooking Time: 60 min.

1. Heat the coconut milk in a large saucepan over low heat.
2. Add the shallots, garlic and ginger. Cook for 5 minutes.
3. Add the chicken to the pan and turn up the heat until it is evenly browned on all sides.
4. Add the curry powder and turmeric and stir well to evenly coat the chicken.
5. Add the rice and soy sauce. Stir well.
6. Pour in 1 c. water and stir well.
7. Add pods, bay leaf and cinnamon stick.
8. Cover and bring to a boil.
9. Reduce heat and simmer gently for 35 minutes or until the rice is tender.
10. Remove from heat and let sit for 10 minutes with the lid on.
11. Fluff the rice with a fork and discard the bay leaf, pods, and cinnamon stick. Serve warm.

- 60ml. coconut milk
- 1 shallot, finely chopped
- 2 cloves garlic, finely chopped
- 1 tbsp. fresh ginger, finely chopped
- 4 chicken breasts, skinned, boned
- 1 tbsp. curry powder
- 1/4 tsp. turmeric
- 10.5 oz. basmati rice
- 1 tbsp. low-sodium soy sauce
- 4 cardamom pods
- 1 bay leaf
- 1 cinnamon stick

Percent Daily Values (DV) are based on a 2000 calorie diet.

Calories	159.4	Protein	11.4g
Total Fats	2.0g	Potassium	166.0g
Sodium	106.2mg	Phosphorus	12.8%

169 | THAILAND

Made in the USA
Lexington, KY
04 May 2015